W9-BNO-200

Praise for *Solving Tough Problems*

"Many people have written about the healing power of dialogue. None, however, has put that power to the test under more extreme conditions with greater success than Adam Kahane. Informative, inspiring, and beautifully written. Highly recommended."

—David Korten, President of the People-Centered Development Forum, and author of *When Corporations Rule the World*

"This generative dialogue approach offers real opportunities for governments to engage with stakeholders to build trust and create exciting new resolutions to multi-faceted social and governance challenges."

—Clare Beckton, Assistant Deputy Attorney General of Canada

"Adam Kahane's book invites us to dare to move back into that sacred space of silence: a space where we listen and hear with our hearts, and not only with our heads. The stories he tells celebrate the amazing transformation that takes place when we have the courage to be vulnerable and speak openly and honestly—where passion is not used to defend an ideology or position, but is directed at enhancing a shared commitment for a common purpose. This is a book that needs to be read now."

—Njongonkulu Ndungane, Anglican Archbishop of Cape Town

"Adam Kahane presents a very strong case for how authentic dialogue can change the world. A fascinating mix of both large ideas and practical details, winnowed from decades of experiences in many countries and institutions around the world. A definitive work on a transformational social innovation."

—Nicanor Perlas, recipient of the Right Livelihood Award (Alternative Nobel Prize), and author of *Shaping Globalization: Civil Society, Cultural Power, and Threefolding*

"A brave and powerful book."

—Len Lindegren, former Global Strategy Leader, PricewaterhouseCoopers

"This fascinating book paints both seemingly unsolvable problems and a path towards sustainable solutions. A 'must read' for those who want to be part of creating such new realities."

Jeroen Bordewijk, Senior Vice President, Unilever

"Being successful in business today means being able to solve complex challenges in a dynamic global environment, while building teams that can handle change creatively. This book shows us how to unlock the creativity of diverse teams to find solutions that work."

—Katherine Taylor, Director General, General Electric Medical Systems Mexico

"This book makes a strong case, from fascinating inside stories about the really tough problems in the world, that success depends on leaders learning to listen. Recommended reading for all decision takers dealing with tough problems."
—Arie de Geus, former Group Planning Coordinator, Royal Dutch/Shell, and author of *The Living Company*

"A book that needs to be read everywhere people have differences—in politics, the church, labor, the academy, and business. Kahane's message is wise, honest, and above all realistic. A gift for our time."
—W. Brian Arthur, Citibank Professor, Santa Fe Institute

"This is a profound and important book. It is special in both the simplicity and authenticity of the writing, and the value and far reaching impact of its message. It offers a ways of thinking and acting that can heal the woundedness of our organizations and our communities. I recommend it wholeheartedly."
—Peter Block, author of *Flawless Consulting, Stewardship, The Empowered Manager, The Answer to How Is Yes,* and *Freedom and Accountability at Work*

"Adam Kahane has written a useful and powerful book. It turns out that the rational, structured approach is just the beginning. Success occurs only when people deeply listen and talk with each other."
—Harrison Owen, author of *Expanding Our Now, Tales from Open Space,* and *Open Space Technology*

"Adam Kahane is one of those all too rare 'warriors for peace' who is willing to immerse himself totally into our world's most intractable conflicts. In story after story, we witness the remarkable transformation of isolated individuals—separate, hostile, closed to one another, with fixed positions—into a single, complex, organism with a common goal, fresh thinking, and, most of all, hope. Kahane makes it crystal clear that deep talking and listening do not come easily, but when they do, the world moves."
—Barry Oshry, author of *Seeing Systems: Unlocking the Mysteries of Organizational Life* and *Leading Systems: Lessons from the Power Lab*

"Kahane puts into words wisdom glimpsed from the cauldron of real world experience. He renews our hope that it is possible to map a better future and sustains our faith that the heart can be a guide."
—Alan Briskin, author of *The Stirring of Soul in the Workplace*

"This book is a gem—in a class of its own. It explains simply and eloquently the essence of the process of non-violent, voluntary transformational change in social systems that seem stuck in hopelessness."
—Arun Maira, Chairman, The Boston Consulting Group India

"This book is a victory for those of us who believe that even the most intractable of our societal problems can be successfully addressed through the efforts of people of good will. It inspires us with real stories of unlikely groups of people separated by gulfs of fear, history, rage and violence, sitting down and bridging chasms of mistrust through the simple human acts of speaking and listening from the heart. I recommend it highly."

—Robert Gass, Rockwood Leadership Program;
former President, ARC International

"This book includes the story of the Visión Guatemala team, in which a group of us, who in the ordinary course of events would never have met or worked together, had an unprecedented experience that opened up new horizons for us and for our country. Adam helped us cultivate our dreams and ideals, and gave us the energy and hope to act to renew our society."

—Raquel Zelaya, former Secretary of Peace, Guatemala

"I have facilitated dialogue and problem-solving in many of today's 'intractable' conflicts—Cyprus, the Caucasus, Kosovo, and Colombia, among others. This book offers valuable new approaches for working in these situations. It goes beyond dialogue, and offers ways of building on dialogue to create new realities."

Diana Chigas, Conflict Management Group and
Fletcher School of Law and Diplomacy

"Tough problems is an understatement. This book provides a road map for solving the intractable and the tragic. Companies facing extinction, communities on the brink, and countries in crisis—Kahane has used his tools in all these contexts, and serves them up admirably in this volume."

—Michel Gelobter, Executive Director, Redefining Progress

"This book offers us stories of profound transformation—and with a refreshing directness teaches us ways of talking and listening that can embrace the toughest problems. The packing of so much practical wisdom into such a small space creates a jewel of inspiration."

Betty Sue Flowers, Director, Lyndon Baines
Johnson Presidential Library

"Adam Kahane is one of those rare action-intellectuals who combines a deep theoretical understanding of social change and group process with actual experience in situations of conflict and turmoil, where people are desperate for solutions but unable to secure what they need. Adam brings the catalyst for change."

—James Garrison, President of State of the World Forum
and author of *America as Empire*

"At the heart of many of our most intractable problems lies the belief that reflection and action are somehow separate. *Solving Tough Problems* goes a long way in healing this rift. In doing so it elegantly sets out a direction for us to follow if we are to shift radically our current destructive patterns of behavior."

—Zaid Hassan, Cultivation Unit, Pioneers of Change

"This is a book about miracles, not the kind of miracles produced by angels but the kind produced by people listening and talking to one another. When faced with tough, complex problems such conversations are likely to be more helpful than yet more 'objective' analyses."

—David Brooks, Founding President, Friends of the Earth Canada

"Adam Kahane pens his mind and heart in prose reminiscent of personal letters to an intelligent friend. His theme is simple and admirable: how to replace the power of violence with the power of listening-and-talking, of regenerative dialogue. His stories move me, unveiling, as no other book, how the informed and reflective heart is the essential compliment to rational, strategic thought."

—Peter Warshall, editor, *Whole Earth,*
the magazine of the *Whole Earth Catalog*

"The world we live in requires that we all take responsibility for the good of the whole; our collective future depends on it. Adam Kahane has given us a lovely treatise on how that can happen individually and collectively through open minds and open hearts."

—Carolyn Lukensmeyer, President and Founder, America*Speaks*

Solving Tough Problems

Solving Tough Problems

An Open Way of Talking, Listening, and Creating New Realities

Adam Kahane

BERRETT-KOEHLER PUBLISHERS, INC.
San Francisco

Berrett-Koehler Publishers, Inc.
235 Montgomery Street, Suite 650
San Francisco, CA 94104-2916
Tel: (415) 288-0260   Fax: (415) 362-2512
www.bkconnection.com

Ordering Information
Quantity sales. Special discounts are available on quantity purchases by corporations, associations, and others. For details, contact the "Special Sales Department" at the Berrett-Koehler address above.
Individual sales. Berrett-Koehler publications are available through most bookstores. They can also be ordered directly from Berrett-Koehler: Tel: (800) 929-2929; Fax: (802) 864-7626; www.bkconnection.com
Orders for college textbook/course adoption use. Please contact Berrett-Koehler: Tel: (800) 929-2929; Fax: (802) 864-7626.
Orders by U.S. trade bookstores and wholesalers. Please contact Publishers Group West, 1700 Fourth Street, Berkeley, CA 94710. Tel: (510) 528-1444; Fax (510) 528-3444.

Berrett-Koehler and the BK logo are registered trademarks of Berrett-Koehler Publishers, Inc.

Printed in the United States of America
Berrett-Koehler books are printed on long-lasting acid-free paper. When it is available, we choose paper that has been manufactured by environmentally responsible processes. These may include using trees grown in sustainable forests, incorporating recycled paper, minimizing chlorine in bleaching, or recycling the energy produced at the paper mill.

Library of Congress Cataloging-in-Publication Data
Kahane, Adam.
  Solving tough problems : an open way of talking, listening, and creating new realities / Adam Kahane.
    p. cm.
  Includes bibliographical references and index.
  ISBN-10: 1-57675-293-3; ISBN-13: 978-1-57675-293-7
  1. Conflict management. 2. Problem solving. 3. Communication. I. Title.

HM1126.K34 2004
303.6'9—dc 22

                                                                2004046130

First Edition
10 09 08 07 06   10 9 8 7 6 5 4

Interior Design: Gopa and Ted2 Design   Proofreader: Henrietta Bensussen
Copy Editor: Judith Brown   Indexer: Medea Minnich
Production: Linda Jupiter, Jupiter Productions

To my family

Contents

Foreword by Peter Senge

*I*NCREASINGLY WE FACE ISSUES for which hierarchical authority is inadequate. No CEO can transform a company's ability to innovate, or single-handedly create a values-based culture. No country president can resolve intractable political stalemates that stand in the way of national development. It is painfully apparent that even the most powerful political leaders and global institutions are powerless in the face of issues like climate change or the growing gap between rich and poor that, if left unaddressed, will undermine the future we leave our children and grandchildren.

Faced with this reality, we see everywhere a growing sense of powerlessness and an increasing reliance on force. The former reflects awareness that the big issues are generally getting worse, not better; the latter, a desperate response to this awareness. Few of us do not shudder at the prospect of a continuation of today's escalating reliance on force. Adam Kahane's book poses a third option: a transformation in our ability to talk, think, and act together. I am convinced this is the only reliable path forward, not only for hierarchical leaders but for all of us—as parents, citizens, and people at all levels in organizations—seeking to contribute to meaningful change.

While this third option is commonly dismissed as idealistic and unrealistic, Adam's belief in this possibility has been forged in the fire of some of the world's most complex and conflicted situations. As a young scenario planner from Shell, he found himself in 1991 helping formerly outlawed black political party leaders in South Africa develop strategies to guide their divided country. The problem was that they saw the world differently from one another and very differently from the white minority with whom they had to work. Remarkably, in little more than a year, this Mont Fleur scenario process resulted in a meaningful consensus on many of the country's core challenges and a way of talking and working together that united a broad cross section of the country. South Africa still faces immense challenges, but it is hard to imagine the country's transition to stable multiracial democracy without this process and others like it.

Since then, many similar experiences—some successful and some not—have illuminated a few simple principles around which Adam's story unfolds.

We are unable to talk productively about complex issues because we are unable to listen. Politics and politicians today epitomize virtually the opposite of the symbol from which their calling emerged—the Greek *polis*—where citizens came to *talk together* about the issues of their day. Things are little better in most corporate boardrooms, where the most difficult and politically threatening issues often never see the light of day. Indeed, we now have a new hero of corporate governance: the "whistleblower" who risks it all to say what no one wants to hear.

Listening requires opening ourselves. Our typical patterns of listening in difficult situations are tactical, not relational. We listen for what we expect to hear. We sift through others' views for what we can use to make our own points. We measure success by how effective we have been in gaining advantage for our favored positions. Even when these motives are covered by a shield of politeness, it is rare for people with something at stake truly to open their minds to discover the limitations in their own ways of seeing and acting.

Opening our minds ultimately means opening our hearts. The heart has come to be associated with muddled thinking and personal weakness, hardly the attributes of effective decision makers.

But this was not always so. "Let us bring our hearts and minds together for the good of the whole" has been a common entreaty of wise leaders for millennia. Indigenous peoples around the world commence important dialogues with prayers for guidance, in order that they might suspend their prejudices and fears and act wisely in the service of their communities. The oldest Chinese symbol for "mind" is a picture of the heart.

When a true opening of the heart develops collectively, miracles are possible. This is perhaps the most difficult point of all to accept in today's cynical world, and I will not try to argue abstractly for what Adam illustrates so poignantly. By miracles I do not mean that somehow everything turns out for the best with no effort or uncertainty. Hardly. If anything, the effort required greatly exceeds what is typical, and people learn to embrace a level of uncertainty from which most of us normally retreat. But this embrace arises from a collective strength that we have all but ceased to imagine, let alone develop: the strength of a creative human community grounded in a genuine sense of connectedness and possibility, rather than one based on fear and dogma.

It has been my privilege to work with Adam for the past decade, as part of a growing community of intrepid explorers around the world looking for alternative paths to catalyze and sustain profound, systemic change. This work is being done in corporate, governmental, and nongovernmental organizations, and in settings that involve all three sectors. It is a joy to see some of the initial articulations of its foundations now reaching publication.

Through this time I have come to appreciate Adam as a consummate craftsman, a deeply pragmatic person not given easily to hyperbole or naïve expectations. This book captures his spirit as well as his knowledge. The theory and method gradually emerging from this collective work sit quietly in the background of his story of challenges, accomplishments, failures, and discoveries.

Although what Adam and others of us are learning is undoubtedly no more than first steps, I believe the direction is becoming clear. The path forward is about becoming more human, not just more clever. It is about transcending our fears of vulnerability, not finding new ways of protecting ourselves. It is about discovering how to act in service of the whole, not just in service of our own interests. It is about rediscovering our courage—literally, *cuer age,* the rending of the heart—to pursue what Adam calls "an open way," because the only progress possible regarding the deep problems we face will come from opening our minds, hearts, and wills.

Peter M. Senge
Cambridge, Massachusetts
April 2004

Acknowledgments

I WOULD LIKE TO acknowledge the kind help I have received in writing this book: from my colleagues, especially Joseph Jaworski, Otto Scharmer, Susan Taylor, and the late Bill O'Brien; from my readers and editors, especially Valerie Andrews, Janet Coleman, Elena Diez Pinto, Kees van der Heijden, Betty Sue Flowers, David Kahane, Art Kleiner, Steve Piersanti, Bettye Pruitt, and Peter Senge; and from my family, especially Dorothy.

Introduction: The Problem with Tough Problems

*T*OUGH PROBLEMS usually don't get solved peacefully. They either don't get solved at all—they get stuck—or they get solved by force. These frustrating and frightening outcomes occur all the time. Families replay the same argument over and over, or a parent lays down the law. Organizations keep returning to a familiar crisis, or a boss decrees a new strategy. Communities split over a controversial issue, or a politician dictates the answer. Countries negotiate to a stalemate, or they go to war. Either the people involved in a problem can't agree on what the solution is, or the people with power—authority, money, guns—impose their solution on everyone else.

There is another way to solve tough problems. The people involved can talk and listen to each other and thereby work through a solution peacefully. But this way is often too difficult and too slow to produce results, and force therefore becomes the easier, default option. I have written this book to help those of us who are trying to solve tough problems get better at talking and listening—so that we can do so more successfully, and choose the peaceful way more often. I want talking and listening to become a reliable default option.

Problems are tough because they are complex in three ways. They are dynamically complex, which means that cause and effect are far apart in space and time, and so are hard to grasp from firsthand experience. They are generatively complex, which means that they are unfolding in unfamiliar and unpredictable ways. And they are socially complex, which means that the people involved see things very differently, and so the problems become polarized and stuck.

Our talking and listening often fails to solve complex problems because of the way that most of us talk and listen most of the time. Our most common way of talking is telling: asserting *the* truth about the way things are and must be, not allowing that there might be other truths and possibilities. And our most common way of listening is not listening: listening only to our own talking, not to others. This way of talking and listening works fine for solving simple problems, where an authority or expert can work through the problem piece by piece, applying solutions that have worked in the past. But a complex problem can only be solved peacefully if the people who are part of the problem work together creatively to understand their situation and to improve it.

Our common way of talking and listening therefore guarantees that our complex problems will either remain stuck or will get unstuck only by force. (There is no problem so complex that it does not have a simple solution . . . that is wrong.) We need to learn another, less common, more open way.

I have reached these conclusions after twenty-five years of working professionally on tough problems. I started off my career as someone who came up with solutions. First I was a university researcher in physics and economics, and then an expert analyst of government policy and corporate strategy. Then in 1991, inspired by an unexpected and extraordinary experience in South Africa, I began working as a neutral facilitator of problem-solving processes, helping other people come up with their own solutions. I have facilitated leadership teams of companies, governments, and civil society organizations in fifty countries, on every continent—from Royal Dutch/Shell, Intel, PricewaterhouseCoopers, and Federal Express, to the Government of Canada and the European Commission, to the Congress of South African Trade Unions and the Anglican Synod of Bishops—helping them address their organizations' most difficult challenges. And I have also facilitated cross-organizational leadership teams—composed of businesspeople and politicians, generals and guerrillas, civil servants and trade unionists, community activists and United Nations officials, journalists and clergy, academics and artists—helping them address some of the most difficult challenges in the world: in South Africa during the struggle to replace apartheid; in Colombia in the midst of the civil war; in Guatemala in the aftermath of the genocide; in Argentina when the society collapsed; and in deeply divided Israel-Palestine, Cyprus, Paraguay, Canada-Quebec, Northern Ireland, and the Basque Country.

Commuting back and forth between these different worlds has allowed me to see how tough problems can and cannot be solved. I have been privileged to work with many extraordinary people in many extraordinary processes. From these experiences I have drawn conclusions that apply not only in extraordinary but also in ordinary settings. In the harsh light of life-and-death conflicts, the dynamics of how people create new realities are painted in bright colors. Having seen the dynamics there, I can now recognize them in circumstances where they are painted in muted colors. I have learned what kinds of talking and listening condemn us to stuckness and force, and what kinds enable us to solve peacefully even our most difficult problems.

My favorite movie about getting unstuck is the comedy *Groundhog Day*. Bill Murray plays Phil Connors, a cynical, self-centered television journalist who is filming a story about Groundhog Day, February 2, in the small town of Punxsutawney, Pennsylvania. He despises the assignment and the town. The next morning, he wakes up to discover, with horror, that it is still February 2, and that he has to live through these events again. This happens every morning: he is stuck in reliving the same day over and over. He explains this to his producer Rita, but she laughs it off. He tries everything he can in order to break this pattern—getting angry, being nice, killing himself—but nothing works. Eventually he relaxes into appreciating the present, and opens himself up to the town and to Rita. Only then does he wake up to a new day and a better future.

Many of us are like Phil Connors. We get stuck by holding on tightly to our opinions and plans and identities and truths. But when we relax and are present and open up our minds and hearts and wills, we get unstuck and we unstick the world around us. I have learned that the more open I am—the more attentive I am to the way things are and could be, around me and inside me; the less attached I am to the way things ought to be—the more effective I am in helping to bring forth new realities. And the more I work in this way, the more present and alive I feel. As I have learned to lower my defenses and open myself up, I have become increasingly able to help better futures be born.

The way we talk and listen expresses our relationship with the world. When we fall into the trap of telling and of not listening, we close ourselves off from being changed by the world and we limit ourselves to being able to change the world only by force. But when we talk and listen with an open mind and an open heart and an open spirit, we bring forth our better selves and a better world.

Tough Problems

PART I

"There Is Only One Right Answer"

*W*HEN I WAS YOUNG, I thought that the world's toughest problems would be solved by the world's smartest people, and I wanted to be one of them. So in 1978, when I started university at McGill in my home town of Montreal, I chose honors physics. This degree involved courses only in theoretical physics and advanced mathematics—nothing but the laws of nature and of pure reason.

My classmates and I were proud to be inducted into this elite intellectual fraternity. We trained by reproducing an increasingly difficult series of logical proofs. Our textbooks contained questions at the end of each chapter and the answers at the back of the book. Our quantum physics course was graded based on a single open-book exam. Before the exam I worked through every exercise in the text, and so I got a perfect grade.

We understood that there is only one right answer.

During the summers, I had electronics jobs in different laboratories. When you're troubleshooting circuits, either the wires are connected properly and it works, or not: you're completely in control. One weekend I went horseback riding, and I was concerned with how to get the horse to raise its leg to get over a log, when—without any instructions from me—the horse did it! I was not used to dealing with living, sentient systems.

One year, while I was still a student at McGill, I participated in a meeting of the Pugwash Conference, an association of the world's top scientists dedicated to preventing nuclear war. I had written a paper arguing that airplanes were more ideally suited than satellites to monitor nuclear test ban treaty compliance, because airplanes are cheaper and more flexible. I ignored the practical and legal reasons why this regime would be harder to implement. Bob Williams, a Princeton scientist and policy advocate, pleaded with me not to fall into the idealist's trap of "letting the best be the enemy of the good." I didn't understand his point. Wasn't there only one right answer?

At one of the conference sessions, a woman from Sri Lanka gave a compelling speech about her country's shortage of energy. I liked the idea of using my scientific training to solve complex societal problems. One of the conference participants, physicist John Holdren, ran a graduate program in energy and environmental economics at the University of California at Berkeley, and so in 1982 I moved there.

The Berkeley economics department had a strong theoretical and mathematical orientation. They and I thought that my physics degree was adequate preparation—even though I had not taken any undergraduate courses in economics or other social sciences—because their mathematical models of economic behavior treated people like predictable, inert objects. I discovered that economists are only slightly less confident than physicists that they possess objective truths about the way the world works. When their truths were questioned during the recession of the early 1980s, my professors were embarrassed and distraught. "This really isn't a good time for you to study macroeconomics," one counseled.

At Berkeley I reoriented myself from solving tough physics problems to solving tough public policy problems. I learned to be a policy "wonk": I'd analyze a societal problem, calculate the right solution, write a paper on it, and then advocate for government decision makers to implement it. I built a computer model of the Canadian economy to assess the impact of different ways to tax energy and to critique the government's policies.

I wrote my thesis on the Brazilian government's program of substituting alcohol for gasoline. After reading every report written about the program, I concluded that it was misguided.

My classmates and I fought for more rational energy and environmental policies. In our second year seminar, "Tricks of the Trade," John Holdren taught us how to testify before a congressional committee—our idea of the ultimate decision makers—and to give a sharp answer on the spot: "That's an excellent question, Senator. The answer is 10.7 exajoules. That's why I recommend that you vote in favor of this legislation." We were learning to be "policy doctors": to make a dispassionate diagnosis and write out a policy prescription, which the decision makers would take and implement and which would cure the problem.

Once I had my degree from Berkeley, I took a series of economics research jobs, first at the Lawrence Berkeley Laboratory in Berkeley, then at the International Energy Agency in Paris, the Institute for Energy Economics in Tokyo, and finally at the International Institute for Applied Systems Analysis (IIASA) in Vienna. Set up during the Cold War, IIASA brought scientists from the East and West blocs to work together, apolitically, on complex global challenges such as population pressure, global warming, and energy shortages.

The institute had a relaxed, intellectual atmosphere. In the mornings we were served Viennese pastries with coffee. In the afternoons there were lectures from resident and visiting scholars. I set out to work on the biggest, toughest problem I could find. I was going to calculate, by hand, a "general equilibrium" model of the interactions among energy, capital, labor, and technology in the world economy. I wanted to prove mathematically the optimum level of world energy consumption. This would indicate the correct policies that the world's decision makers should implement for energy supply, pricing, and conservation. This problem turned out to be more difficult than I expected. I spent week after week covering sheet after sheet of paper with formulae, getting more and more confused and frustrated. Eventually it dawned on me that the problem was probably mathematically insoluble and, more devastatingly, that nobody had any interest in or use for any solution I might find. I had completely floated away from earthly reality.

This realization led me, when I returned to the United States in 1986, to look for a "real job." I got one at Pacific Gas and Electric Company in San Francisco, the monopoly supplier of electricity and natural gas to Northern California. PG&E was right in the middle of pitched analytical and political battles over nuclear power, environmental protection, energy conservation, and utility deregulation. I was given the title Corporate Planning Coordinator and an office near the top executives, with a beautiful view of San Francisco Bay. My job was to work on strategic problems and recommend solutions to the executives. I understood that the way to get ahead was to know the one right answer to any question, quickly: "Well, boss, the return on that investment would be 10.2 percent. So I recommend that we go for it."

PG&E, a publicly traded company, was strictly regulated by the California Public Utilities Commission (CPUC). The company had a simple, highly controlled business model: it forecast what it needed to do in order to serve its ratepayers, added up these "revenue requirements," and then petitioned the CPUC for permission to charge rates sufficient to cover them. These regulatory rules were designed to provide consumers with reliable, low-cost energy, and to provide PG&E shareholders with a low but steady rate of return. The primary focus of PG&E's management attention was therefore not on customers, but on formal public hearings before the CPUC. Fittingly, eight of the nine members of the company's executive Management Committee were lawyers.

In our semijudicial rate hearings before the CPUC, we asked for rate increases to cover the cost of investing in new power plants to meet growing consumer demand. Our case rested on the soundness of our forecasts. Consumer and environmental groups tried to prove that our forecasts were too high and that we did not really need to build more power plants or have higher rates. We had a set of sixteen detailed, linked mainframe computer models that took ten days to run through. At the CPUC hearings, energy policy experts fought "model wars" as to who had the right numbers about the future; in other words, who had the societally optimal answer.

After a year, this whole approach started to seem like make-believe to me. From my work on forecasting at IIASA and before, I knew that no one could really have the right numbers about the future—especially because deregulation was about to upend the industry. This orderly, controlled edifice of models and predictions and hearings was not realistic.

In the midst of all of these changes and challenges at PG&E, I was very content to be working directly for the real decision makers. I reported to the Senior Vice President of Corporate Planning, Mason Willrich, a former law school professor and an arms control policy expert. I was delighted with my boss, and I could only imagine how much more brilliant *his* bosses must be. The hierarchy at PG&E was so obvious that it was never even mentioned. The CEO was in charge, his senior officers were next in line, and then the officers, and so on down the ranks. I assumed that the people at the top were smarter and more informed than the rest of us.

I was keen to fit in and make a good impression. On my first day I mentally measured the width of Willrich's trouser leg where it hit his shoe, so that I could make sure mine did the same. After only a few weeks, I found myself smiling every time I walked past a PG&E manhole cover on the sidewalk. I was happy to be doing an important job for an important company.

Because I coordinated internal planning studies for the Management Committee, I went to some of their meetings in the enormous, oak-paneled boardroom on the top floor. Here, conversations were polite, reasoned, and completely under control. The company secretary provided orderly agendas and discreetly negotiated minutes.

In my second year, I was assigned to assemble the analytical material for the annual Management Committee strategy retreat. The meeting was held at a rustic lodge on a wild mountain property, near one of the company's small hydroelectric dams. I was excited to be with the bosses in their inner conclave, even though on the first evening, the president took several hundred dollars away from me in a poker game.

Given my exalted expectations, the retreat itself was a profound letdown. I watched the business sessions in stupefied disbelief. The executives ignored the analytical material, played power games, ganged up on each other, pretended to misunderstand, settled old scores. I was deeply disillusioned and felt my commitment to the company slipping away. This was not at all the brilliant, informed, rational decision making that I had been trained to expect. The world did not work the way my one-right-answer textbooks said it did. Something much messier was really going on—and I wanted to understand it.

Seeing the World

*I*N 1988 I LEFT PG&E and took a job in the
strategic planning department of Royal Dutch/
Shell, the giant Dutch-British energy and chemicals company:
almost 100 years old, $100 billion in sales, and over 100,000
employees in more than 100 countries; the fourth largest industrial company in the world. The global petroleum business was
much different from the California utility business. Shell was not
concerned with regulatory hearings; it was dealing with the hurly-
burly of the marketplace. It was wonderfully cosmopolitan, intellectual, and practical: a combination of British subtlety and
Dutch bluntness. If Shell staff were arrogant, I thought, it was
because they deserved to be: they were the best. Here I could learn
how the world really worked.

My job was to come up with new ideas that would provoke,
stretch, and challenge the managers' thinking about tough business problems—to improve the quality of their strategic debates.
From the window of my office in the London headquarters, I
could see the Houses of Parliament. Like Parliament, Shell
believed in the value of debate to hammer out a sound way forward. And like "Her Majesty's Loyal Opposition," our department
had to ask the difficult and awkward questions that would challenge the managers and improve the quality of their thinking.

Our primary tool for this challenging was scenarios. Our leader
was Dutchman Kees van der Heijden, a rigorously thoughtful man
who had worked with Pierre Wack, the philosophical Frenchman

who had invented this approach in the early 1970s. Shell could neither predict nor control the future of its business environment, and it was therefore impossible for us to compute one right strategy for the company. Instead, the company's managers needed to be alert to what was happening and what might happen in the world, so that they could quickly recognize meaningful changes and adapt to them. Our scenarios were a set of carefully constructed, plausible stories about how the future might unfold over the next twenty years.

Wack's methodology was sophisticated and expansive. He called the first phase of the work "breathing in." We observed the world, as broadly and carefully as we could, looking for underlying trends. We had wide-ranging interests: the future of the nation state, environmental science, automobile technology, social values, Middle East economics, the politics of international trade. I found this a wonderful intellectual adventure and an amazing education. We read books and journals, commissioned and wrote research papers, and organized expert seminars.

The most important way we learned about the world was to go out and talk with people. We had a blank check to go anywhere and meet anyone who could help us see the trends more clearly. The purpose of these meetings was not only to learn what was going on but also how different people thought about it. I talked with civil servants in the UK and Belgium, businessmen in Singapore and Brazil, environmentalists in Kenya and Germany, journalists in Thailand and India, academicians in China and Czechoslovakia, politicians in Korea and Nigeria, engineers in Japan and the United States.

After two years of breathing in, we were ready to breathe out. We spent months arguing about the significance of what we had seen and how it added up. I enjoyed these debates and played to win. Eventually we selected two scenarios that effectively and elegantly synthesized what we had learned about what might happen in the company's business environment. Then we wrote these scenarios up in the form of plausible, logical, quantified stories.

The management decisions of Shell were never included in the stories: we assumed that the company's actions had no impact on the scenarios.

Next, we flew around the world, with our thick deck of view-graphs, to run workshops for every management team in the company. We challenged each team to study the two scenarios and consider what each, were it to occur, would mean for their business. What specific opportunities and threats would arise in their markets? Which of their unit's strengths and weaknesses would be exposed? What actions would be indicated? We wanted the managers to "live in advance" and internalize these different possible futures. We did not want them to operate from a single fixed view of what they thought would or should happen. In this way, every unit in Shell adjusted its strategy so as to be more robust against both of these stories.

One of our global scenarios focused on climate change. I was proud of this work because I was concerned about environmental problems. This helped Shell managers see and recognize the importance of these issues earlier than competitors, and to take the lead in sustainable development. As far as I was concerned, Shell was doing a good job in the world. But I was now more pragmatic, even cynical. I was far beyond the naïve idealism that had brought me to Berkeley. I now knew that every trend had a countertrend, every argument had a rebuttal, and every solution produced a new problem. I knew that there was no longer one right answer. My world had become more realistic—and more complex.

In 1990, van der Heijden retired from Shell. He was replaced by Joseph Jaworski, an outside hire with a markedly different background and orientation. Jaworski was a successful Texan trial lawyer and businessman who had spent the 1980s founding and building the American Leadership Forum, a nonprofit organization dedicated to strengthening collaborative civic leadership in the United States. He was innovative and curious. He was not an expert in global scenarios and did not mind admitting it. He was also intensely idealistic, which set his pragmatic colleagues, including me, on edge.

We started to develop a new set of global scenarios. After the fall of the Berlin Wall, we focused on the twin revolutions of political and economic liberalization and globalization. We constructed two new stories—named *New Frontiers* and *Barricades*—about how the world might unfold as a result of these dynamics. *New Frontiers* described what happens when poor countries liberalize successfully and claim a larger role on the world stage. This opening up is turbulent and painful to many established interests in both poor and rich countries, but it continues because people believe that it is in their long-term self-interest. In *Barricades,* people resist globalization and liberalization because they fear they might lose what they value most: their jobs, power, autonomy, religious traditions, and cultural identities. Economic and political vested interests are deeply threatened by opening up, and they attempt to contain it.

These new scenarios raised a new set of tough business problems for Shell managers to address. And they had a significantly different twist that was elicited by Jaworski's visionary and activist orientation. He and I and a few other members of the scenario team were convinced that *New Frontiers* would be better for the world than *Barricades,* and that Shell should, in addition to preparing for both scenarios, actively promote *New Frontiers.*

Some people in our department thought that this would not be right. Favoring one story over another would make managers less adaptable in the face of uncertainty. Furthermore, companies should not intervene in politics; they should stick to running businesses.

I was intrigued by this debate about the appropriate role of Shell in the world. I understood the reasons for detached observation and challenge, and why Jaworski's activism did not quite fit in. Shell's business managers were responsible for creative, entrepreneurial action; our department's job was just to challenge these managers' thinking. I also understood the risks of corporate hegemony, and that many citizens would view any attempts by Shell to act outside its business role with skepticism and hostility. At the same time, the company's belief—"we are just business people, we observe what is going on and try to adapt, within laws and rules that governments set"—struck me as somewhat disingenuous and self-serving, even irresponsible. Shell, one of the world's largest and most powerful organizations, was in general a beneficiary of the way the world's rules had been written, and actively lobbied for its specific interests in economic, energy, and environmental rule making. I wondered whether there wasn't a different, more engaged way for the company to participate in solving complex problems.

Jaworski's passionate and idealistic activism challenged my dispassionate and realistic scientific training. He looked for evidence of the better future he intuited and hoped was possible and then acted entrepreneurially to bring this vision into reality. I admired his whole-hearted commitment and leadership. And I was surprised to discover that my own desire to make a difference, which had faded after I left Berkeley and entered the "real world," was returning.

The Miraculous Option

*I*N THE MIDDLE OF 1991, Jaworski was in his office at Shell when he received a telephone call from Pieter le Roux, a professor at the left-wing, black University of the Western Cape in South Africa.

One year before, the white minority government of F. W. de Klerk had released Nelson Mandela from prison after twenty-seven years, and simultaneously legalized all the black opposition parties, including Mandela's African National Congress (ANC). This broke a deadlock in one of the world's most stuck political situations. Now the government and the opposition were trying to do what nobody believed could be done: negotiate a peaceful transition from an authoritarian apartheid regime to a racially egalitarian democracy.

Le Roux wanted to organize a scenario project to help the opposition develop its strategy for this unprecedented transition. South Africa had had two previous scenario projects, both of which had been sponsored by big South African companies and advised by Pierre Wack, by then long-retired from Shell. Le Roux liked the idea of using a corporate methodology for "the world's first scenario planning exercise of the left." He also wanted an advisor from Shell and so called Jaworski to ask for one.

Shell executives were still smarting from the criticism they had endured during the years when their products had been boycotted internationally because of Shell's investments in South Africa. And Jaworski was keen to find ways for the company to get engaged in creating *New Frontiers*. It was therefore agreed that I would provide methodological advice to the project team and facilitate their scenario workshops. This sounded interesting to me, and so in September 1991 I flew from London to Cape Town for the project's first workshop.

The workshop venue was the Mont Fleur Conference Center on a wine estate in the mountains just outside Cape Town. Le Roux had assembled a group of twenty-two influential South Africans. He had invited leaders from all the main groups within the left-wing opposition: the ANC, the radical Pan-Africanist Congress (the PAC, which had not yet renounced their "armed struggle"), the powerful National Union of Mineworkers, and the South African Communist Party. He had also, daringly, invited some of their longtime adversaries from the white business community and academia. The team therefore represented, unofficially, parts of both the existing establishment and the establishment-to-be— a microcosm of the future South Africa.

The experience of constructing Shell-type scenarios in a group dominated by leftist African activists was an adventure for the participants and for me. Trevor Manuel, head of the ANC's Economics Department, introduced me to the group as "a representative of International Capital."

I could see that this scenario meeting was not going to be like the Shell ones I was used to. We were not working on an ordinary problem of organizational strategy but on an extraordinary national transformation. The team members had not come to the meeting because they had been told to or because it was their job, or because they or their satisfied organizations wanted to adapt as best they could to an uncertain future. They came because they were all deeply dissatisfied with the status quo and committed to changing it. They saw this project as an opportunity to participate in giving birth to the "New South Africa."

The composition of the team had two benefits for our scenario work. First, the team wouldn't have to seek out other people in order to accomplish their core scenario-building task—"breathing in" the reality of South Africa from multiple perspectives—because most of the key perspectives were already represented. Secondly, le Roux had begun the project with the endorsement of three top black leaders: Thabo Mbeki of the ANC, who later succeeded Mandela as president of the country; Anglican Archbishop Desmond Tutu; and Deputy President Dikgang Moseneke of the Pan-Africanist Congress. So we already had links to the opposition leaders whose strategies we were trying to inform.

The team started off in mixed small groups, brainstorming possible scenarios for South Africa over the decade ahead. I asked them to use the Shell convention and to talk not about what they or their party wanted to happen—their usual way of talking about the future—but simply about what might happen, regardless of what they wanted. Each small group could present back to the whole group any story they wanted, as long as they could argue that it was logical and plausible. The listeners in the plenary were not permitted to shout down the story with "That couldn't happen" or "I don't want that to happen." They could only ask "Why would that happen?" or "What would happen next?"

The team found this scenario game to be fabulously liberating. They told stories of left-wing revolution, right-wing revolts, and free market utopias. They told some politically incorrect stories, such as "Growth through Repression" (a play on words on the left's slogan of "Growth through Redistribution"), in which a Chilean-type authoritarian government produces strong economic growth. They also rejected as implausible some politically correct stories, such as one in which the People's Republic of China provides the military support that enables a victorious socialist insurrection in South Africa.

The workshop was taking place just after the white government had relaxed its "petty apartheid" restrictions on social interaction. The scenario team was excited to be able to work together across white-black, establishment-opposition lines. Many of them were meeting for the first time, and the relaxed, residential setting helped them to get to know one another. We had the whole of the beautiful Mont Fleur center to ourselves. During breaks in the workshop we went for walks on the mountain or played volleyball or billiards. In the evenings we had long conversations in the lounge, which had a well-stocked wine cellar sponsored by one of the participating companies. I chatted by the fireplace with Dorothy Boesak, a black community leader who was coordinating the project. This whole scene was remarkable for many reasons, but especially because only a few years before, South African laws would have prohibited any such socializing between whites and blacks.

The first brainstorming exercise produced thirty stories. The team combined these and narrowed them down to nine for further work, and set up four subteams to flesh out the scenarios along social, political, economic, and international dimensions. The subteams worked from September through December, when the whole team reconvened at Mont Fleur for a second workshop. They first addressed the nine scenarios in more depth and then narrowed the field to four that they thought, given the current situation in the country, were the most plausible and important. After that workshop, the team went back to their own organizations and networks to test these four scenarios. At a third workshop, in March 1992, the participants reviewed and refined the write-ups of the final scenarios and agreed how they would be published and disseminated. Finally, in August, the team held a fourth, one-day workshop—with a four-hour break in the middle so that participants could watch an important rugby game— to present and test the logic of the scenarios with a broader and more senior group, including politicians from the white liberal Democratic Party, the right-wing Conservative Party, and the governing National Party.

The team's final scenarios asked the question: How will the South African transition go, and will the country succeed in "taking off"? Each of the four stories gave a different answer and had a different message that mattered to the country in 1992. South Africa was in the middle of the contentious and risky transition negotiations. Nobody knew how or even whether they would succeed, or if the country would remain stuck, closed, embattled, and isolated. As a set, the scenarios provided a provocative road map for this transition. There were three dark prophecies of futures to avoid: *Ostrich*, in which the nonrepresentative white government sticks its head in the sand to try to avoid a negotiated settlement with the black majority; *Lame Duck*, in which there is a prolonged transition with a constitutionally weakened government which, because it purports to respond to all, satisfies none; and *Icarus*, in which a constitutionally unconstrained black government comes to power on a wave of popular support and noble intentions, and embarks on a huge and unsustainable public spending program, which crashes the economy. Then there was one bright vision of a future to work towards: *Flight of the Flamingoes*, in which the transition is successful because all the key building blocks are put in place, with everyone in the society rising slowly and together.

Once the four scenarios had been agreed upon, the team introduced them into the national conversation. They inserted a twenty-five-page booklet into the leading weekly newspaper, arranged for the work to be discussed in the media, and distributed a cartoon video of the four stories. Most importantly, they ran more than 100 workshops for leadership groups of their own and other influential political, business, and civic organizations, where the four scenarios were presented and debated. President de Klerk reacted to Mont Fleur by saying, "I am not an Ostrich."

Icarus got the most attention. Here the leading economists of the left were warning their comrades of the dangers of irresponsible left-wing economic policies. Mosebyane Malatsi of the Pan-Africanist Congress, the ANC's main rival on the left, presented *Icarus* to his own top leaders. He said, "This is a scenario of what will happen if the ANC comes to power. And if they don't do it, we will push them into it." Malatsi was showing his colleagues both an unfamiliar and undesirable economic scenario for South Africa and the role that their own policies and actions would play in such a scenario. His presentation produced a long, intense, self-critical discussion among the PAC leaders. Soon after this meeting, the PAC changed their economic policies and then decided to abandon their armed struggle and join the constitutional negotiations.

A similar shift in thinking occurred among the top leaders of the ANC. Trevor Manuel and his deputy Tito Mboweni led the presentation to this group, which included Nelson Mandela, Oliver Tambo (president of the ANC), and Joe Slovo (chairperson of the South African Communist Party). At the time, the ANC's leadership was focused primarily on achieving a political, constitutional, governmental, and military transition. Their economic thinking, formed during the Cold War and the South African guerrilla war, was tightly held. Their general view was that the country was rich and that an ANC government could simply redistribute money from rich whites to poor blacks. *Icarus,* presented at this meeting by their own top two economists, was therefore a direct attack on the party's orthodoxy. When some participants demurred, it was Slovo, citing his personal experience with failed socialist programs in the Soviet Union and elsewhere, who argued that *Icarus* needed to be taken seriously.

The economic message of Mont Fleur affected ANC thinking profoundly. Derek Keys, minister of finance in the de Klerk government, attended the fourth Mont Fleur workshop, and one evening he offered to share some material from a briefing on the economy he had just given to the de Klerk cabinet. Manuel and others said they were interested, and a long conversation ensued. Reporter Patti Waldmeir later described it this way:

> Keys gave ANC economics head Trevor Manuel a briefing on the economy, and Manuel repeated it to Mandela. "And I got frightened," Mandela recalls. "Before Trevor finished, I said to him, 'Now what does this mean as far as negotiations are concerned? Because it appears to me that if we

allow the situation to continue . . . the economy is going to be so destroyed that when a democratic government comes to power, it will not be able to solve it.'" Mandela made a decision—the deadlock [in the then-stalled negotiations on a post-apartheid political order] must be broken.

So Mont Fleur helped to shift the economic thinking and acting of the ANC and other left-wing parties and to avert an economic disaster. One of the most important surprises and successes of the post-1994 ANC government has been its strict and consistent fiscal discipline, as articulated in the 1996 Growth, Employment, and Reconstruction (GEAR) policy. In his history of this transition, Allister Sparks refers to this fundamental (and still controversial) change in economic policy, incubated at Mont Fleur, as "The Great U-Turn." In 2000, seven years after the project ended, Trevor Manuel, who by then had succeeded Keys as the country's first black minister of finance, had this to say:

> It's not a straight line [from Mont Fleur to GEAR]. It meanders through, but there's a fair amount in all that going back to Mont Fleur . . . I could close my eyes now and give you those scenarios just like *this*. I've internalized them, and if you have internalized something then you probably carry it for life.

Businessman and political analyst Vincent Maphai, one of the convenors of Mont Fleur and an intimate observer of the ANC cabinet, said, "Trevor Manuel and Tito Mboweni are aimed at one thing: preventing the *Icarus* scenario." In 1999, Mboweni, at the official banquet for his inauguration as the country's first black governor of the Reserve Bank, reassured his audience of local and international bankers by saying, "We are not *Icarus*; there is no need to fear that we will fly too close to the sun."

Looking back, South Africans have since 1994 been on a slow, steady, collaborative ascent: a *Flight of the Flamingoes*.

I was delighted and fascinated by all of these impacts of the Mont Fleur team's work. This was the first time that I had descended from observing complex problems from above and outside as a researcher and corporate planner, to engaging right up close with a group of people who were in the middle of working through solutions. Their process did not work the way I expected it to. There were no clever viewgraphs or brilliant experts or anonymous decision makers in the picture. The stories had played a part in solving an important set of national problems, but they were really quite simple, even simplistic—not nearly as sophisticated and carefully thought through as our Shell scenarios.

The essence of the Mont Fleur process, I saw, was that a small group of deeply committed leaders, representing a cross-section of a society that the whole world considered irretrievably stuck, had sat down together to talk broadly and profoundly about what was going on and what should be done. More than that, they had not talked about what other people—some faceless authorities or decision makers—should do to advance some parochial agenda, but what they and their colleagues and their fellow citizens had to do in order to create a better future for everybody. They saw themselves as part of—not apart from—the problem they were trying to solve. The scenarios were a novel means to this engaged problem-solving end.

The Mont Fleur scenario team had used the same methodology as the Shell team, but for a fundamentally different purpose. At Shell we built scenarios to improve our managers' ability to adapt to whatever happened in the future. At Mont Fleur, by contrast, the team built scenarios not only to understand what was happening and might happen in the future, but also to influence and improve the outcome. At Shell we were observers and reactors; at Mont Fleur, team members were actors. The Mont Fleur team's fundamental orientation—and the primary message they gave to the leadership groups they engaged with—was that more than one future was possible and that the actions they and others took would determine which future would unfold. The team did not believe they had to wait passively for events to occur. They believed they could actively shape their future. They understood that one reason the future cannot be predicted is that it can be influenced.

This was the same point that Jaworski had been making to our team at Shell. In his book *Synchronicity: The Inner Path of Leadership,* Jaworski later wrote:

> If individuals and organizations operate from the generative orientation, from possibility rather than resignation, we can create the future into which we are living, as opposed to merely reacting to it when we get there.... All human beings are part of that unbroken whole which is continually unfolding from the implicate and making itself manifest in our explicate world. One of the most important roles we can play individually and collectively is to create an opening, or to "listen" to the implicate order unfolding, and then to create dreams, visions, and stories that we sense at our center want to happen.... Using scenarios in this way can be an extraordinarily powerful process—helping people to sense and actualize emerging new realities.

At Mont Fleur the team was not only doing something essentially different from anything I had ever seen, but they were doing it with an oddly different spirit. They were working on big, serious issues over which they had been engaged in life-and-death struggles for decades. But they were doing this openly, creatively, and lightheartedly, having fun with their ideas and with each other.

My own stance as a facilitator helped. I joined the Mont Fleur team with what was, for me, an exceptional orientation. In the weeks preceding the first workshop, I had been busy with my Shell work and so did not have time to prepare as I usually would have: reading up on South Africa and then, on the long flight from London to Cape Town, composing my expert view on what the country and the team ought to do. I also did not know much about the members of the team, except that they were a heroic group, many of whom had been beaten, jailed, or exiled for their work. I was, therefore, both neutral and respectful—which turned out, unintentionally and synchronistically, to be the perfect recipe for being a facilitator. The more I worked with the team, the more impressed I became with them, and as I opened up, this inspired reciprocal opening by them. One team member later said to me, "When we first met you, we couldn't believe that anyone could be so ignorant. We were sure that you were trying to manipulate us. But when we realized that you really didn't know anything, we decided to trust you." Both the team and I were able, at least for a while, to give up knowing and take up learning.

For me, the Mont Fleur process was a revelation and awakening. I knew that I had witnessed something unusual and important—a Grail—even though I wasn't sure exactly what it meant. I had walked through a doorway, even though I wasn't sure what was on the other side. I had fallen in love with this way of working on the toughest of problems, with the vitality and open-heartedness of South Africans, and also with Dorothy Boesak. It was all quite jumbled up in my mind, but I did not have to decide what to do. I knew. In 1993, I resigned from Shell, emigrated to South Africa, and married Dorothy. I exchanged the controlled neatness of my Shell, London, bachelor life for the messiness of self-employment, in a country undergoing a revolution, with a wife and four teenage stepchildren.

Dorothy and I had a joyful wedding at the Mont Fleur Conference Center. Many of the team members, pleased to have been party to the romance, were there. It was a real New South Africa affair: my Jewish family from Canada, Dorothy's family and her Dutch Reformed minister, a Xhosa marimba band, a Zulu singer, a Muslim jazz pianist. Although the day was mostly a blur, I distinctly remember turning and facing the guests just after we had said our vows and feeling an unexpected, overwhelming wave of love engulfing all of us. At that moment, the whole tent full of people seemed one,

The Mont Fleur experience left me with two questions. First, Why was the Mont Fleur work unusual and important? Observation and reflection revealed the answer to this question over the following months. Second, How had the team members done this work? I could only come up with an answer to this question from the inside, subjectively, as a participant in the work, and it came to me gradually over the ten years that followed.

The South Africa that I traveled to in 1991 and 1992, and moved to in 1993, was a country between regimes. The 1980s had ended in a stalemate: both the white minority government and the radical opposition had tried to win by force, and both had failed. In 1990, de Klerk broke the stalemate by releasing Mandela and legalizing the opposition groups, but the country's first all-race elections were not held until 1994. This four-year transitional period was a roller coaster of euphoric highs and bloody lows, agreements and assassinations, breakthroughs and breakdowns.

South Africa's system of governance during this period was extraordinary. The old order was dying, but the new order had not yet been born. There were no agreed rules for making national decisions. The de Klerk government was formally in charge, but its legitimacy and power were slipping away, and it had to consult the ANC on most major issues. Just after I immigrated in 1993, for example, the popular black politician Chris Hani was assassinated by a white conservative, and de Klerk, fearing a black uprising, had to rush Mandela onto national television to appeal for calm.

In this governance vacuum, South Africans were cobbling together a variety of ad hoc processes. The most prominent and visible of these was the series of official conferences among the political parties to negotiate a political settlement and a new constitution, complete with scrupulously balanced delegations, position papers, and formal rules of order. But less visible were hundreds of "forums," covering every imaginable issue and scale:

the National Housing Forum, the National Education Forum, the Orange Free State Drought Committee, the Western Cape Regional Economic Development Forum, and many others. Each of these forums had its own idiosyncratic structure and process, but all of them brought together the actors with a stake in a particular problem—from government, opposition parties, companies, trade unions, community groups, universities, and so on—to develop a shared understanding of the problem and to find ways to solve it. These actors participated in the forums because they believed they were facing problems that none of them could solve alone through ordinary, established processes. They therefore needed these extra-ordinary, multi-stakeholder, dialogue-and-action processes.

The forums became the mechanism through which specific transitional agreements were reached. Equally important was their function as the mechanism through which a cross-sectoral network of trusting relationships—what Robert Putnam calls "social capital"—was built. The dramatic overall political and constitutional settlements that South Africans achieved in 1994 rested on the relationships they built through these many dialogic processes. The Mont Fleur project was both an example and a part of this larger problem-solving process.

A popular joke at the time said that, faced with the country's daunting challenges, South Africans had two options: a practical option and a miraculous option. The practical option was that we would all get down on our knees and pray for a band of angels to come down from heaven and fix things for us. The miraculous option was that we would continue to talk with each other until we found a way forward together. In the end, South Africans, contrary to everybody's predictions, succeeded in implementing the miraculous option. Forums like Mont Fleur were miracle-implementing processes.

My key insight was that South Africans had discovered an exceptionally effective way to solve tough problems. I proved this to myself with the painstaking logic of an ex-physicist. I knew that problems are tough because they are complex, and that there are three types of complexity: dynamic, generative, and social.

A problem has low *dynamic* complexity if cause and effect are close together in space and time. In a car engine, for example, causes produce effects that are nearby, immediate, and obvious; and so, why an engine doesn't run can usually be understood and solved by testing and fixing one piece at a time. By contrast, a problem has high dynamic complexity if cause and effect are far apart in space and time. For example, economic decisions in New York affect the price of gold in Johannesburg, and apartheid-era educational policies affect present-day black employment prospects. Such problems—management theorist Russell Ackoff calls them "messes"—can only be understood systemically, taking account of the interrelationships among the pieces and the functioning of the system as a whole.

A problem has low *generative* complexity if its future is familiar and predictable. In a traditional village, for example, the future simply replays the past, and so solutions and rules from the past will work in the future. A problem has high generative complexity if its future is unfamiliar and unpredictable. South Africa, for example, was moving away from the peculiar rigidities of apartheid and into a new, post–Cold War, rapidly globalizing and digitizing world. Solutions to problems of high generative complexity cannot be calculated in advance, on paper, based on what has worked in the past, but have to be worked out as the situation unfolds.

A problem has low *social* complexity if the people who are part of the problem have common assumptions, values, rationales, and objectives. In a well-functioning team, for example, members look at things similarly, and so a boss or an expert can easily propose a solution that everyone agrees with. A problem has high social complexity if the people involved look at things very differently. South Africa had the perspectives of black versus white, left versus right, traditional versus modern—classic conditions for polarization and stuckness. Problems of high social complexity cannot be peacefully solved by authorities from on high; the people involved must participate in creating and implementing solutions.

My analysis gave me a neat answer to my first question: Why was the Mont Fleur work unusual and important? Simple problems, with low complexity, can be solved perfectly well—efficiently and effectively—using processes that are piecemeal, backward looking, and authoritarian. By contrast, highly complex problems can only be solved using processes that are systemic, emergent, and participatory. The Mont Fleur approach was important and unusual because it was exceptionally well suited to solving highly complex problems—to enacting profound social innovations. Our process was *systemic,* building scenarios for South Africa as a whole, taking account of social, political, economic, and international dynamics. It was *emergent,* because it recognized that precedents and grand plans would be of limited use, and instead used creative teamwork to identify and influence the country's critical current choices. And it was *participatory,* involving leaders from most of the key national constituencies. The mother of this South African invention was the necessity of its transitional vacuum: a highly complex system, in a fundamentally new context, in which no single authority had the wisdom or legitimacy to enforce solutions. With the practical option of intervention from "above" unavailable, South Africans had no choice but to rely on the miraculous option of working together.

My analysis also allowed me to recognize a widespread "apartheid syndrome." By this I mean trying to solve a highly complex problem using a piecemeal, backward-looking, and authoritarian process that is suitable only for solving simple problems. In this syndrome, people at the top of a complex system try to manage its development through a divide-and-conquer strategy: through compartmentalization—the Afrikaans word *apartheid* means "apartness"—and command and control. Because the people at the bottom resist these commands, the system either becomes stuck, or ends up becoming unstuck by force.

This apartheid syndrome occurs in all kinds of social systems, all over the world: in families, organizations, communities, and countries.

South Africa is in many ways a microcosm; the country is, as Allister Sparks observes,

> where the First and Third Worlds meet, . . . the developed and developing worlds, the dark-skinned and light-skinned worlds, the rich and the poor, in the same proportions as the rest of the global village of roughly one to five. It is where the white-skinned First Worlders tried to keep the dark-skinned Third Worlders out of their islands of affluence in the cities with pass laws and influx control regulations, just as the developed nations try to stop them from crossing the global poverty barriers of the Rio Grande, the Mediterranean, and the Pacific Rim, and with as little success.

Apartheid could not be sustained in South Africa, and it cannot be sustained elsewhere—except by force. Everywhere, people are struggling to overcome their own apartheids. They are struggling to find peaceful ways to solve their own highly complex problems. The lessons of the South African transition and of Mont Fleur are therefore relevant to many other contexts.

This realization brought me back, with even greater interest, to my second, unanswered question: How had the Mont Fleur team members done their work? The only way I was going to understand this was to immerse myself in this work and observe the people who were doing it up close.

Soon I would have many opportunities to do just that.

Talking

PART II

*I*N 1993, AFTER I LEFT SHELL and moved to South Africa, I started Generon Consulting. My partners were Joseph Jaworski, who by then had also finished his assignment at Shell, and Bill O'Brien, the former president of Hanover Insurance. Later Otto Scharmer of the Sloan School of Management at the Massachusetts Institute of Technology joined us as a research partner. The Mont Fleur approach became well known, and teams of people all over the world—in and across companies, governments, and civil society organizations—asked us to help them work on their most important and difficult problems.

Through this work, I gradually, over the next decade, pieced together an answer to my second question, which I came to think of as: How can we solve tough problems peacefully? The answer turned out to be both simple and practical: by opening up our talking and listening. With that insight, I can look back and see the key pattern across all the projects my colleagues and I have worked on. At one extreme, some projects were characterized by completely closed talking and listening, and these ended up getting stuck or getting dealt with by force. Other projects were characterized by completely open talking and listening, and these succeeded in creating new realities. Most projects fell somewhere between these two extremes. I have laid out the stories in this book in this opening-up order, rather than chronologically. Each chapter that follows illustrates and explains one degree of greater openness than the chapter before. This progression offers a theory and practice of how to solve tough problems.

Through this work, I also gradually pieced together how to do my job as a process facilitator. A friend once sent me an email with this message: "How does one learn good judgment? Experience. And how does one gain experience? Bad judgment." My hard-won experience has taught me that I also am least effective when I am closed and most effective when I am open. But this simple opening-up turned out to be far more subtle and challenging than I would ever have imagined.

Being Stuck

*S*OUTH AFRICA had been stuck in apartheid for decades, but by the time I first went there in 1991, South Africans were in the middle of changing that. What does a tough problem look like when it is still stuck in the apartheid syndrome?

It looks like the Basque Country did in October 2002. When I went there to share my South African experiences, Basque nationalists were fighting for independence from Spain, or at least for the right to vote on it. Non-nationalists and the Spanish government wanted the Basque Country to remain part of Spain. Over the previous five years, this conflict had grown increasingly polarized and violent. The nationalist terrorist group ETA (Euzkadi to Askatasuna, which means "Basque Homeland and Freedom" in the Basque language) had killed more than 850 people and planted bombs in Bilbao, Madrid, and tourist resorts, so that hundreds of public officials needed full-time bodyguards. The police had killed 170 people and made more than 11,000 arrests. The Basque Country was thoroughly stuck and therefore increasingly dangerous. As one local peace researcher explained to me, "A conflict that does not move positively, moves negatively."

I met with partisans and politicians from all sides. I found them gracious and hospitable, but also frightened, guarded, angry, and frustrated. They were all keen to tell me their stories: ETA killed my husband; Franco's soldiers killed my mother's father; the nationalists are trying to intimidate us; the Spanish are trying to erase our culture. They all explained why they were the victims and the others were the villains.

I noticed how much less willing the parties were to talk with each other than with me. The Spanish government had just outlawed the ETA-linked political party, Batasuna, on the grounds that it was a front for terrorists, and had broken off all political contact with the nationalist Basque regional government on the grounds that the Basque problem required a police rather than a political solution. The premier of that regional government had just put forward a plan for a referendum on quasi-independence and said that he would implement it with or without the cooperation of the Spanish—which the Spanish prime minister promptly denounced as the ranting of a fanatic. Amplifying the conflict, each side's media allies demonized their opponents and denounced anyone who met with the other side. Nobody could get all the parties to talk together directly. Even Elkarri (the Basque word for "together"), a grassroots peace organization, could only succeed in getting some of the parties to talk, and those only through intermediaries and in private. Even so, after a year, they could not get agreement even on a one-page public statement on a process for moving towards peace.

Gorka Espiau, an Elkarri staff member, explained to me the interaction between violence and nondialogue: "If I know that you, my opponent, would approve of my being killed, that you do not have a basic respect for human life, then how can I have an open, human dialogue with you? And yet without such a dialogue, how can we end the violence? We have to start with a political dialogue to reach an agreement to stop the killing. Then we can have the human dialogue that we need to resolve the deeper underlying conflict."

I met with an opposition member of the Basque regional legislature who told me that the violence had now undermined all communication among the politicians. Once-cordial working relationships in the parliament had broken down into acrimonious exchanges and stony silences. After this meeting, I went upstairs to sit in the visitor's gallery to watch the parliamentary debate. One member was giving an impassioned speech about a crucial legal aspect of the conflict. In the half-empty chamber, not one of the other members was listening to him: they were talking on their cell phones, reading newspapers, dealing with their correspondence, napping. I asked the usher if it was usually like this. "Yes," he answered. "The members usually make up their minds before the debate as to how they are going to vote, and so they don't need to listen to the speeches."

The Basque premier said two things that allowed me to glimpse the costs of being stuck and the benefits of getting unstuck. He told me a story that I had heard from other Basques on both sides: "The conflict here is not between different tribes or ethnic groups. Many of our families are split down the middle between nationalists and non-nationalists. When my brothers and sisters and I go home to our parents for Christmas, my mother begs us not to talk about politics. It's a terrible feeling, as though I have to cut off a part of myself." Later, when I asked him what it had been like being premier during 1998 to 1999, when ETA had declared a cease-fire, his face became wistful: "You can't imagine what it was like for me to be able to hear a telephone ring without fearing that it would be news of another bombing or assassination. That was such a wonderful time in Basque society: an emotional blossoming."

In each of my meetings, I talked about the South African transition and about Mont Fleur and the many other informal forum-style meetings among all the parties. The Basques were intrigued —they had never had an all-party meeting—but pessimistic. "That might be useful here," each of them responded, "but I don't think it would be possible. I'm not sure that they would be willing to talk with us, and we're not really ready to talk with them." (About such stalemates, Nelson Mandela once said, "One effect of sustained conflict is to narrow our vision of what is possible. Time and again, conflicts are resolved through shifts that were unimaginable at the start.")

This pattern of not talking and not listening is a symptom of being stuck. Whether or not the actors are on speaking terms, they are not on listening terms. Like the Basque parliamentarians (and many parliamentarians elsewhere), they have made up their minds before their opponents speak. Even if they are silent and pretending to listen, they are really only "reloading," rehearsing their rebuttals. They are in fact listening only to themselves, to the tapes they play over and over in their heads about why they are right and others are wrong. My partner Otto Scharmer calls the kind of talking that takes place in these situations "downloading" because the speaker is reproducing an old file without alteration. The actors sometimes fight openly and violently, and sometimes cover their differences with politeness, skirting sensitive subjects in order to keep the peace. Either way, they are stunted, unable to express who they are in new ways and unable to take in what others are telling them. If they can change this pattern and start to talk and listen, they blossom.

Not talking and not listening are common; they are not limited to troubled nations. As I drafted this chapter, my twenty-seven-year-old daughter Pulane and I were enacting this same pattern. She was home for the holidays and had stayed out all night without telling Dorothy and me where she would be. So we fought about her "irresponsibility" and my "interference," downloading an argument we had had on and off for years. Each of us knew with certainty that we were right and the other was wrong. "If she won't listen to me telling her that she is wrong," I thought, "then why should I bother to talk to her? And if she is going to continue to talk nonsense about my being wrong, why should I bother to listen to her?" Sometimes we yelled, and sometimes we politely avoided the subject. In our own way, we were as stuck as the Basques.

There are two ways to try to unstick a stuck problem. The first is for one side to act unilaterally—to try imposing a solution by force or violence. In the Basque Country, ETA, the Spanish government, and the Basque government were each, in their own way, trying to do this.

The second way to unstick a problem is for the actors to start to talk and listen in order to find a way forward together. South Africans arrived at their dialogue reluctantly and only after both sides had discovered that they were unable to force their solution on the other. Pulane and I also eventually grew out of our fighting: our love for one another prevented us from walking away and encouraged us to keep trying to communicate. But, as of this writing, the actors in the Basque Country are not yet ready to talk and listen. The situation is not ripe enough. Dialogue cannot be forced, and so peacemakers must wait patiently for an opening.

Dictating

*I*N ORDER TO UNSTICK a stuck problem peacefully, the people involved in the problem have to talk with and listen to one another. But there is more than one way of talking and listening, and some ways hardly help at all.

I observed such hardly helpful communication in the problem-ridden context of Paraguay. Paraguayans seem to enjoy telling awful and bizarre stories about their country. The first evening I was there, in 2001, a presidential candidate boasted to me about the suicidal War of the Triple Alliance (1864–1870), in which Paraguay battled its three much larger neighbors, Brazil, Argentina, and Uruguay, and lost half of its people. Men had to be imported to re-grow the population. "We are," he concluded with a flourish, "a fierce and crazy people."

Their recent history has been similarly awful. General Alfredo Stroessner was elected president in 1954 and stayed in power for thirty-five years through siege, harassment, murder, political purges, and bogus elections. His overthrow in 1989 released a wave of excitement and optimism. Then resignation set in again. Many of the country's institutions are corrupt. A Paraguayan CEO told me that the majority of his law school class did not study because they had purchased their degrees in advance. At the time, he was fighting a trumped-up fraud case in the Supreme Court in which his opponent had paid off several of the judges. A journalist told me that the president of Paraguay drives a stolen car and that the president of Uruguay had his watch stolen off the lectern when he gave a speech to the Paraguayan Congress.

"An optimist in Paraguay," someone quipped, "is someone who says, 'Things are good! We are better off today than we will be tomorrow!'"

I went to Paraguay to work with forty-five of the country's most open-minded and public-spirited politicians, activists, businesspeople, generals, judges, journalists, intellectuals, peasants, and students. They had agreed to talk together, but I was puzzled by how slowly our work progressed. Most of them seemed to be exceptionally suspicious, cynical, and pessimistic, and hesitant about speaking openly. They deferred to me even on questions for which I had no good answers. Conversations went in circles; understandings came unraveled; commitments were not kept.

I spoke about these patterns with Milda Rivarola, a member of the team and a respected historian. "You have to understand the impact that the dictatorship had on people," she explained. "We needed approvals and permissions for everything. No criticism of the government was allowed. The only way to have influence was to be a part of the government, the military, or the governing party. And by and large people acquiesced. Stroessner had a network of spies and informers (many of them had volunteered!) who set people against each other. Just like in other totalitarian and post-totalitarian societies, social fragmentation was and is severe. What you are seeing in this group—the low levels of trust and initiative—are the after-effects of this repression."

The director of our project was a civic leader named Jorge Talavera, who had worked for decades in adult education and leadership development. He was sanguine about the situation and patient with our slow progress. "Paraguayans aren't used to managing themselves," he explained. "They are always asking 'Who's the boss?' People say that President Wasmosy, our first civilian president after Stroessner, used to assert his authority by asking, 'Who's the penis here?' In this project we are asking people to value their own experiences and to have confidence that they can influence the future. So we are asking them to make a fundamental shift in their way of being. This will take time."

In a dictatorship, the dictator does not listen, and the people are afraid to talk. The results are pessimism and cynicism; lack of self-confidence and self-management; hesitation to speak up and stand up; and painfully slow innovation.

Now that I have seen this pattern of behavior in Paraguay, where it was painted in bright colors, I am able to recognize it elsewhere. Today I see it in most organizations, where bosses give orders and employees are afraid to say what they think. Just compare what people say in meetings with their bosses to what they say outside the meetings, in the HERD (a corporate colloquialism for *h*allways, *e*levators, *r*estrooms, and while *d*riving). A long-suffering civil servant in Mexico told me a joke about a government minister who asks one of his officials if crocodiles can fly. "No minister," the official replies. The minister then says, "I think that they can." "You're right, minister," the official quickly replies, "but *very* close to the ground." This joke could be told about the bosses and subordinates in most of the organizations I have worked with.

The root of not listening is knowing. If I already know the truth, why do I need to listen to you? Perhaps out of politeness or guile I should pretend to listen, but what I really need to do is to tell you what I know, and if you don't listen, to tell you again, more forcefully. All authoritarian systems rest on the assumption that the boss can and does know the one right answer.

I had never noticed the parallel between political dictatorship and organizational authoritarianism because authoritarianism was the water I had always swum in. When I joined Pacific Gas and Electric, it never occurred to me to question the strict reporting lines. Until I attended the Management Committee's retreat, I had assumed that the bosses at the top were smarter and so rightfully at the top. Furthermore, I had always had elite jobs, close to the bosses, and the degenerative consequences of authoritarianism are hard to see from the top. It was only later, when as a consultant I interviewed both bosses and their employees, that I realized how much more oppressive these systems look and feel from below.

Another reason I had not seen the parallel between dictatorship and authoritarianism is that I had always assumed that dictators had to brutalize people in order to shut them up. Then I read an essay by Tina Rosenberg about Chile under General Augusto Pinochet:

> Chileans had never been submissive and sycophantic, but it was not hard to learn. If a man lost his job for refusing to attend a Pinochet rally, the next month his neighbor went to the rally and even brought along a banner to wave. If silence was required to keep a job, stay out of jail and maybe even receive a bag of toys at Christmas, Chileans were silent.
>
> But there were in Chile, as there are everywhere, always, people who are not easily silenced. For such people, other means of intimidation were employed: torture and death. Pinochet used fear surgically, applying it in just the degree necessary for the task at hand, taking care not to rouse from their sleep those Chileans who preferred not to know what was going on ...
>
> A shrewd dictator does not crush everyone. How much better to simply seduce: provide people with quiet streets, imported autos, or the luxury of having someone else do their thinking for them, in exchange for their silence and subservience. Dictatorship did not just coerce Chileans; it also corrupted them.

Organizational authoritarianism also produces silence and subservience, through coercion, seduction, and corruption. I once worked on an innovation project with the management team of a successful Fortune 100 communications company. Its founder and CEO was a brilliant man, and a bully. His very highly paid senior managers admired and feared him. They spent a lot of their time looking over their shoulders, worrying about how to keep him happy and panicking when they heard that he wasn't. They would second-guess themselves, skirting areas where they knew he had strong views, start down one path, and then suddenly change course if he frowned on it.

This is the corporate version of the apartheid syndrome: management of a complex system by force and fear. Business writer Harriet Rubin once said to me that it surprised her that people were willing to accept being free citizens on the street but serfs at work.

The communications company's managers replicated the CEO's style with their subordinates. And I was shocked to realize how easily I slipped into doing the same, ratcheting up my cagy politicking and authoritative expertness, which only served to reinforce the patterns of behavior that were holding back the innovation that our project was intended to stimulate. The company continued to be successful only because its business system was highly centralized and because the CEO continued to dictate excellent, systemwide strategies. One employee, who had worked with these senior managers for decades, said, "They have no energy; they have turned into turnips. They don't want to do anything. They like having excuses. They are all making big salaries and feeling no pain. They have the perfect cover for anything: 'Our bosses won't let us do anything.' There was a time when they had spirit, but they have been emasculated. Their spirit has been sucked out of them."

This description of the communications company managers echoes Rosenberg's description of the Chileans. I have noticed that many of the people in many of the systems I have worked with—including the presidents, CEOs, and generals—say these same words: "The people above me won't let me do anything." This is a symptom of the pervasiveness and internalization of authoritarianism.

The authoritarian approach to solving problems is that the boss, with his smart expert advisors and consultants, dictates solutions. For simple problems, this works wonderfully. Unilateral decision making is fine for a police officer directing traffic at a busy intersection. This problem has low dynamic complexity (cause and effect in the intersection traffic are nearby, immediate, and obvious), low generative complexity (traffic rules from the past apply perfectly well), and low social complexity (all the drivers share the same objective of smoothly running traffic and willingly defer to the officer's authority).

But the authoritarian approach does not work for solving complex problems. Consider a global computer company trying to sell into Eastern Europe in the early 1990s, just after the fall of the Berlin Wall. The CEO cannot successfully dictate the company's sales strategy. The development of the computer market is affected by decisions that are being taken far away (in Silicon Valley) and long ago (by Communist industrial planners), and so the sales "problem" has high dynamic complexity that can only be grasped as a whole—for which the CEO needs to think together with the company's front-line staff who are directly in touch with different parts of the system. The problem situation, in the midst of both political and technological revolutions, also has high generative complexity, which means that there is not one right answer that can be created in advance; the situation can only be addressed by working with it as it unfolds. And the problem has high social complexity because it can only be solved with the participation of the people who are part of the problem: global and local staff, customers, suppliers, government officials, and so on.

Unfortunately, the authoritarian approach, with its severe limitations, is the foundation of practically all private and public sector strategic planning. Strategists direct, and others follow. Kees van der Heijden, my former boss at Shell, noted that most of the literature on strategic planning

> falls into "the rationalist school," which codifies thought and action separately. The tacit underlying assumption is that there is one best solution, and the job of the strategist is to

get as close to this as possible, within the limited resources available. The strategist thinks on behalf of the entire organization, and works out an optimal strategy as a process of searching for maximum utility among a number of options. Having decided the optimal way forward, the question of action (known as the "implementation issue") is addressed. . . . The (somewhat unlikely?) assumptions underlying the rationalist school are: predictability, no interference from outside; clear intentions; implementation follows formulation (thought independent of action); full understanding throughout the organization; and reasonable people will do reasonable things.

This emperor-has-no-clothes description of the rationalist school accurately summarizes the approach I learned at Berkeley and applied at PG&E. My training at Berkeley was to use pure reason to come up with the one right answer, as I did on Canadian and Brazilian energy policies. My job as a PG&E planner was to come up with the optimal strategy for the company, convince my boss and the Management Committee to approve it, and then somebody else would implement it.

The authoritarian pattern of talking is that bosses and experts talk down—dictating and telling—and everyone else talks cautiously. This is the closed way. To solve complex problems, we have to find a more open way.

Talking Politely

*I*N ORDER TO SOLVE tough problems peacefully, people must be willing to talk openly. In Paraguay and in the communications company, people hesitated to speak openly because they were afraid of authoritarian reprisal. In Canada, my native country, I worked on a project in which I noticed a different kind of hesitancy—people hesitating to speak openly because they were afraid of offending someone, or of being embarrassed.

We Canadians are polite. It is not that we do not have the same conflicts and passions as other people, just that we prefer not to talk about them. As Canadian novelist Margaret Atwood once said, "Just because English Canadians don't move their faces much doesn't mean they don't have feelings." Sometimes this politeness helps us deal with our challenges, but sometimes it hinders us.

In 1996, I worked with a Canadian team that was trying to make progress on the long-running constitutional tension between Quebec separatists and Canadian federalists (like the Basque conflict, but less violent). Politicians and civil servants had been trying to resolve this issue for decades, without success.

I was coming home, which had disadvantages as well as advantages. I knew more about the country, or at least I assumed I did, and this meant that it was harder for me to listen without rushing to judgments and jumping to conclusions. Being an expert is a severe impediment to listening and learning.

Four federal government civil servants, intelligent and well informed, took the intellectual leadership. Of everyone on the team, they were the ones who had been the most disappointed and embarrassed by previous heartfelt but failed attempts to resolve the conflict. They were therefore cautious, even cynical, about the potential for the team to make a difference. They were also adept at talking about problems dispassionately, conceptually, and politely. I also was more comfortable with this way of talking, and uncomfortable with open, emotional conflict.

The team followed the lead of the five of us, and so conversation remained mostly impersonal, abstract, and calm. From time to time, one of the young people, activists, or entrepreneurs would get excited, but he or she would quickly settle down again. In one session, a doctor declared that alcoholism was a serious problem in aboriginal (Canadian Indian) communities, but his remark was treated with offended indignation, and so he shut up.

There was one particular moment when someone lifted this veil of dispassion. One evening I invited members of the team to tell a story about a personal experience that might illuminate our understanding of the Canadian system. Halfway through this session, a young francophone man from Quebec said this:

> I have to say that when we started this exercise, I thought that with a bit of luck, my turn wouldn't come because we wouldn't have time. In any case, I had decided that I would also like to talk about my family. My father is from Sydbury, Ontario—a Franco-Ontarian. His family had lived there for generations.
>
> His father was a carpenter but my father decided that he liked school and went further in his studies than was the norm in his community and in his family. Eventually, he went to Toronto to pursue his education and his plan, because he realized that Francophones in Ontario were not on an equal footing with Anglophones and all the Francophones he knew were very poor. His plan was to become like an Anglophone,

but he had a hard time of it. Toronto wasn't Sudbury. There were almost no Francophones and he felt very isolated. He couldn't fit into the system, so he flunked out.

Then he moved to Quebec, figuring "I'll go somewhere where Francophones are in the majority," because he thought that Francophones in Quebec must be the ones with the power. He arrived in Montreal and felt like he had been hit by a speeding locomotive. You see, he expected to find a mirror image of Toronto, but in French, and instead he discovered an Anglophone city where all the signs were in English and where it didn't matter what part of downtown you were in, you couldn't get any service in French. At one point he was in despair and saw some graffiti proclaiming "Le Québec aux Québécois" [Quebec for Quebeckers] and from that point on, he became interested in the nationalist debate and in politics.

I've told you this story because it explains to some extent the background of a lot of Quebeckers, the way we perceive Canada. For a variety of historical reasons, Canada has not evolved into the bilingual country we could have hoped for at the start of Confederation [the founding of the country] and I don't think that is something we will ever achieve. Perhaps we have to come up with a plan that is completely different from what was envisaged at Confederation.

I found this story fascinating. Although I had grown up in Quebec, a member of the English minority, I grasped more of the underlying force driving separatism from this five-minute personal story than from twenty-five years of reading newspaper analyses. The story touched other people as well, but I didn't have the presence of mind to recognize its importance. The moment passed, and we continued with our work as before.

The team had unusual difficulty agreeing on a set of conclusions. We had to add an unplanned fifth meeting in order to break the deadlock. Ultimately, we came up with an elegant and abstract set of messages: the country had to adapt quickly to a rapidly changing world; an incremental approach would be dangerous; and success depended less on whether the governance system (including the constitutional arrangement between Canada and Quebec) changed dramatically than on how any change was accomplished.

As soon as our workshops were over, the project fizzled out. Some team members presented our conclusions at conferences and meetings. Then our work was forgotten.

Politeness is a way of not talking. When we are being polite, we say what we think we should say: "How are you?" *"I'm fine."* We do not say what we are really thinking because we are afraid of a social rupture: "How are you?" *"I'm terrible."* When we talk politely, we are following the party line, trying to fit in and so keep the social system whole and unchanged, even though the whole may be diseased or counterfeit. Talking only about concepts is one way of being polite. Usually we are not even aware that we are following rules of politeness, but when we first enter a system with an unfamiliar set of rules—as when I entered PG&E and Shell—we notice them.

Most of the Canadian team were comfortable with the status quo. After all, most Canadians had a good life, there was no war, and few people were exercised by the Quebec-Canada impasse. We were afraid that if the country changed, we might find ourselves in a situation that would be awkward or uncomfortable or dangerous. Unconsciously we therefore kept our conversation safe, conceptual, and polite. The conclusions we agreed on were dispassionate and neutral: we did not take a stand for anything but prudence. Our fear and politeness ended up smothering change. We accomplished the formal objective of the project, but we didn't produce results that anyone cared about.

The young Quebecker stood out because he did not follow these rules. He spoke personally, not conceptually; he was passionate; he took a stand for what he believed in. In these senses he was impolite, which is why his speech was both so jarring and so riveting.

When somebody speaks personally, passionately, and from the heart, the conversation deepens. When a team develops a habit of speaking openly, then the problem they are working on begins to shift. By contrast, a habit of speaking overly cautiously obscures the problem and keeps it stuck. The Canadian team had a hard time agreeing on conclusions because our conversations did not go deep enough for us to find the ground that we truly had in common, and from which we could construct a way forward that we all believed in.

These polite dynamics also play out in ordinary family settings. When my brothers and I go home to see our parents, we all talk politely, staying away from sensitive subjects (or talking about certain subjects only with certain people), keeping things under control. Sometimes I am afraid that if I say what I am really thinking, others will be hurt and upset. I am afraid that I will rupture the family whole—which anyway isn't so bad. So we all say what we always say, replaying the same conversations and the same family reality, over and over. Politeness maintains the status quo.

Most of the meetings I've been in, in organizations of all sorts all over the world, have been polite, like the gatherings of the Canadian team and of my family. Usually this isn't a problem: the issues under discussion are simple and can be dealt with adequately through cautious, dispassionate, amiable talking and listening. But sometimes this kind of conversation is completely inadequate, leaving a dangerous reality unaddressed and unaltered.

The movie *Conspiracy* depicts such a conversation. It tells the real story of a ninety-four-minute meeting on January 20, 1942, at the Wannsee villa outside of Berlin. Kenneth Branagh plays the chairman of the meeting, charming and urbane Reinhard Heydrich, the right-hand man of Heinrich Himmler, head of the SS and the Gestapo. It was at this meeting, held over food, wine, and cigars, that a committee of senior Nazi officials, including Adolph Eichmann, discussed and agreed on the details of Hitler's "Final Solution." I found the movie chilling because it is not melodramatic at all. It seemed to me that I was watching a completely ordinary business conversation. Heydrich calmly and cleverly moves the agenda along. He invites everyone to contribute their views while making it clear, through the kinds of subtle pressure that I have seen in countless meetings, that he is not open to dissent. Although several members of the group have deep reservations about Heydrich's scheme, they want to be seen as "team players," and in the end they go along. The horrible plan is approved.

As long as the status quo is working, we can afford to remain polite. But when we see that the status quo is no longer working, we must speak up.

Speaking Up

*I*N COLOMBIA, the most violent country in the world, the status quo works for almost no one. In proportion to its population, Colombia has the highest number of murders and kidnappings in the world. It has a home-grown academic discipline called violentology. In the first half of the 1900s, it had two bloody civil wars, the second one called simply "The Violence." Since the 1960s it has suffered from an increasingly violent mess of conflicts among the military, drug traffickers, left-wing guerrilla armies, and right-wing paramilitary vigilantes. Yet Colombia has also elected civilian governments for all but 5 of its 185-year history, making it the longest-lasting democracy in Latin America. The country is, like many places, both a disaster and a wonder.

During 1996 and 1997, a team called "Destino Colombia" wanted to use the Mont Fleur approach to find a better way forward for their country. It was then, and as of this writing still is, the only time that all of the armed actors (except the drug traffickers)—plus a diverse group of politicians, businesspeople, and representatives of civil society—met to talk with and listen to one another, and search for a way out of the violence.

We met three times, for ten days in all, at a lovely old farm called Recinto Quirama, in the rolling green hills outside of Medellín. We had the whole spread-out property to ourselves: a high-ceilinged barn for a meeting room, an open-air, cobbled floor dining room and bar, a swimming pool, and simple sleeping rooms surrounded by flower gardens. I arrived a day before the start of the first workshop and was amazed to find such tranquility in the midst of war. Then I went for a swim in the pool and emerged to find the pool surrounded by soldiers with machine guns, there to protect the participants in the meeting from attack.

The most remarkable feature of the project was the participation of both of the illegal, armed, left-wing guerrilla groups: the FARC (the Revolutionary Armed Forces of Colombia) and the ELN (the National Liberation Army). Six months earlier, I had given a speech about Mont Fleur to a meeting in Bogotá. It had been broadcast on shortwave radio so that FARC leaders hiding in the nearby mountains could listen. After I finished speaking, a cell phone rang. It was one of the FARC leaders calling to ask me a question: "Do we have to agree to a cease-fire in order to be able to attend the scenario workshops?" Everybody looked at me, and I gave an answer that I hoped was correct: "The only condition is to be willing to talk and listen." They said that they would come.

Although the government had offered them safe passage to the workshops, the guerrillas thought that this would be too risky, and so they participated by telephone. Three men called in from the political prisoners' wing of the maximum security prison outside of Medellín, and one from an undisclosed hiding place in Costa Rica. This arrangement produced some surreal moments, such as when one of the guerrillas called in from a prison pay phone, saying that he only had enough coins for a few minutes but wanted to offer his input on one of the draft scenarios.

Most of the team members were excited and terrified because they were talking with the guerrillas for the first time. We communicated using two speakerphones in the meeting room. When people walked by the speakerphones, they gave them a wide berth, afraid to get too close. Some of the participants were frightened of retribution for what they might say to the guerrillas. When I mentioned this fear, one of the guerrillas replied, "Mr. Kahane, why are you surprised that people in the room are frightened? The whole country is frightened." Then the guerrillas promised they would not kill anyone for anything said in the meetings.

Once the threat of force had been removed, the team was able to agree to a set of ground rules for their conversations. They agreed to "call things by their name"; to express their differences without irony; to assume the good faith of others; to be tolerant, disciplined, and punctual; to be concrete and concise; and to keep confidences. They were proud of these ground rules because they knew that in the midst of much lawlessness and violence, it was essential to construct a safe space for talking and listening.

Within this cocoon, relationships opened and deepened. During the breaks in the meetings, people now started to huddle around the speakerphones, continuing to talk with the guerrillas. People worked hard all day, then talked and laughed and played guitar in the bar until late at night. I was deeply touched by their heartfelt commitment and communication; it was different from what I had grown up with in Canada.

The team joked about dynamics that were very close to the bone. One morning the representative of the Communist Party overslept after a long evening of singing duets with the retired army general. When he did not show up on time for the meeting, there was a lot of wisecracking about what might have happened to him. "The general made the communist sing," one person said. Then the representative of the right-wing paramilitary said, mock-threateningly, "I was the last one to see him." I was relieved when, a few minutes later, the communist walked into the room.

About half of the participants had lost a member of their immediate family to the conflict. One person's sister had been kidnapped and killed, another's son murdered, another's father assassinated. I was amazed when I realized that these participants were the ones who were most energetic and openhearted in their search for common ground.

As the work progressed, the team became less afraid and more willing to speak frankly. I was particularly struck by one remark. A landowner said that he had had a lot of firsthand experience of the conflict with the guerrillas, that he did not trust them at all, and that he believed that the country's best hope for peace would be to intensify the military campaign against them. Saying this was courageous because he was directly challenging not only the guerrillas but also the rest of the team and their hopeful belief that a negotiated solution was possible. He was willing to be impolite and controversial. But by now relationships were strong enough so that such a statement did not rupture the team. Furthermore, when he said exactly what he was thinking and feeling, the fog of conceptual and emotional confusion that had filled the room lifted, and we could all see an important underlying dynamic in the team and in the country.

This insight made its way into one of the team's published scenarios, *Forward March*. In this story, Colombians, frustrated with failed attempts at peace and intent on rebuilding a broken nation, elect a strong government to impose order through military force, believing that "harsh problems require harsh solutions." Straight talk among the scenario team enabled them to talk straight to the country.

I do not know how or even whether the violence in Colombia will end. The Destino Colombia team succeeded in working together peacefully, but they failed—as all others have—to generate the same dynamic in the country as a whole. A United Nations–sponsored study of the project called it "a treasure still to be revealed." Andres Pastrana, president of Colombia from 1998 to 2002, tried and failed to end the war through negotiation. His successor, Alvaro Uribe, concluded that negotiation could not work and that the country's problems could only be solved by force. He has stepped up the military campaign against the guerrillas—the option described in *Forward March*.

The first step along an open way—the first step out of the apartheid syndrome—is for the actors in the system to speak up. Often this is extremely difficult. People hesitate to say what they are thinking for many reasons, not only extraordinary but also ordinary: fear of being killed or jailed or fired, or fear of being disliked or considered impolite or stupid or not a team player.

Around the time I was working in Colombia, I was taking a part-time master's degree in applied behavioral sciences at Bastyr University in Seattle. I thought that I had gone as far as I could go as a facilitator with an education only in physics and economics, and that I needed some professional training in leadership. I quickly found out that learning to lead means learning how I as a leader function—including my own fear of speaking up.

The core learning process of the program was a kind of awareness training based on the Training Group, or "T Group," pioneered at the National Training Laboratories in the 1960s. In this process, six of us sat in a circle and talked for twenty minutes or so, observed by the teacher and the rest of the class. The only rule was that we could only talk about the "here and now": what we were thinking, feeling, sensing, or wanting at that very moment, in response to what somebody else had just said or to something that was arising within us. This process produced conversations that were utterly banal: "I am feeling flushed and angry after your remark about Mary's tone of voice." At the same time the experience was extremely rich, because in this safe classroom space, we got feedback from our classmates that was immediate and straightforward.

I learned a lot from these T Group sessions about my own patterns of behavior. At the beginning, I tended to hang back, observing and making smart comments. I was told I came across as distant, closed, and condescending—not at all what I wanted. I realized that I was stuck in a personal version of the apartheid syndrome. I hesitated to speak openly because I was afraid that if I said what I was really thinking, the others would be angry and would distance themselves from me, there would be a conflict, and the group would spin out of control and split apart. But I discovered, to my enormous surprise, that the opposite was true: the more open I was, the closer others felt towards me and the closer our group became.

I also learned how my patterns of behavior had their roots in the dynamics of relationships in my family. As a child, I had learned to distance myself from conflict as a way of protecting myself from arguments between my parents. If I wanted to change how I handled such situations now, then I had to relearn these deep-rooted responses, which was hard. This challenge of understanding and changing myself taught me some humility about the prospect of understanding and changing anyone else, let alone a group or larger human system.

In the safe environment of this course, I built up my capacity to speak up and to deal constructively with authority and conflict. I was then able to support the Destino Colombia team in doing the same. Yet even now in many situations, I hold back from saying what I am thinking. It is therefore not surprising that in much more dangerous situations, many people do not have the courage to take the crucial step of speaking up. Often when it is most important for us to speak up, we find it most difficult.

In this context, the conduct of the Destino Colombia team was exemplary. In the heat of terrible conflicts such as Colombia's, many people—if not killed outright—are melted down and destroyed in spirit. But others are raised up and purified. Extraordinary circumstances turn ordinary people into heroes.

The members of the Destino Colombia team who had suffered most directly from the war were the ones who made the most courageous and catalytic statements in the meetings. In the Basque Country, the most outspoken and open person I met was a woman whose husband had been killed by ETA. She was now providing support to victims on both sides of the conflict. "Victims are generous because we have nothing more to lose," she said. "If the politicians would let us, we could be a doorway to a solution."

These people dare to say what they see and think because they believe that their situation demands this of them. They have the courage to overcome their fears of losing what they hold most dear: control, identity, position, power, their life. These people demonstrate to the rest of us what we need to do, in our more normal circumstances—in our families and workplaces and communities—if we want to change the status quo. We must speak up.

Only Talking

_**T**_ALKING OPENLY (as I observed in Colombia) is better than talking guardedly (Paraguay) or politely (Canada) or not at all (Basque Country), in that it allows us to see more of the problem and understand it from multiple perspectives. But by itself, talking about a problem does not change anything. Something more is required.

I learned this when I participated in a series of meetings in the Caribbean. The convenors invited sixty prominent leaders, from all walks of life, to talk about what was going on in the region and what they might do about it. The participants spoke with discouragement about their complex mess of problems: poverty, AIDS, drug trafficking, emigration, political factionalism, economic stagnation, and social deterioration. They also spoke with pride about their democracy and free speech: politicians who argued vigorously in Parliament and in public; newspapers that were full of sharp reporting and serious analysis; and ordinary people who spent hours "reasoning," talking openly and at length in their homes and neighborhoods and on call-in radio programs.

Each participant had a thoughtful opinion and spoke up. But they also felt enormous frustration about so much talking producing such poor results. "There is a view in this country," said one former prime minister, "that if you talk about a problem, you've solved it." One woman, a community organizer, said with great conviction and impatience: "We talk here ad nauseum. But

there is talk and there is talk. Most of our talk doesn't change anything. What would it take for us to really move forward?"

Most conventional approaches to solving problems emphasize
talking, especially the authoritarian, boss or expert, way of talking: telling. In a debate, each party prepares their position and
speech in advance and then delivers it to a panel, which chooses
the most convincing speech. The same process is used in courtrooms and boardrooms, and in parliaments (except that legisla-
tors have usually made up their minds before they hear the
speeches). Experts form ideas and present them, and then authorities adjudicate among these already formed ideas. This approach
works for deciding between already created alternatives, but it
does not create anything new.

The additional element that is required to create something
new, and that is ignored in most conventional approaches, is
listening.

In late 2002, I attended a small conference on the challenges of
globalization. It was a marvelous, diverse group, painstakingly
assembled from around the world: politicians, businesspeople,
activists, and intellectuals. In the context of the impending war
with Iraq, the central, urgent subject was how global problems
could be solved peacefully and how the United States could participate in such a process. The objective was to find ways to create a more equitable system of global governance.

The organizer and chairman of the meeting was a sincere and
considerate American. He convened a series of panels presenting
all perspectives eloquently and provocatively. In the question-
and-answer period, he selected participants from the audience
whom he thought would have something interesting to say and
gave everybody a chance to speak. If he thought that a certain
point of view was being neglected, he would emphasize it himself.

The hot issue of the meeting was the behavior of the United
States. Many participants sharply criticized the country, and some
of the Americans, including one of the meeting's main corporate
sponsors, were defensive. The chairman was frightened that the

Americans would feel uncomfortable and walk out, and so he asked the critics to tone down their remarks. Then he invited the American sponsor to make the final speech of the meeting. The sponsor presented a confident, sweeping survey of the state of the world, complete with 100 PowerPoint slides.

This meeting failed to achieve its objective of creating forward movement towards a new system of global governance. On the contrary, it succeeded inadvertently in exposing our current flawed system in miniature. In a series of orchestrated monologues, all the main points of view were re-presented, with preference given to the famous. The panelists did not listen to each other but merely waited to give their prepared remarks. Everybody could talk, as long as they did not discomfort the powerful. The American sponsor had the final say—and it was a lecture.

The meeting was organized entirely around talking. No attention was paid to listening: to the process of taking in something new and being unsettled and changed by it. The chairman discouraged impoliteness and discomfort. We ended up with a dialogue of the deaf, and the enormous potential of this marvelous group was therefore unrealized. The only forward movement took place outside the meeting room, during breaks and over meals and drinks, when the participants could talk and listen freely. Talk by itself, even brilliant speeches by famous people, does not create new realities. Most of the time it reproduces old ones.

My own behavior at the meeting did not really help. I fell into the same trap that so bothered me in the chairman and the panelists. When I talked with people in the corridors, I gave my same smart speech about how bothered I was by the speechmaking.

This talking without listening is both pervasive and insidious. I once facilitated a workshop of Jewish and Palestinian board members of a civil rights foundation in Jerusalem. The meeting was becoming increasingly tense, and so was I. The more tense I felt, the more directive and forceful my facilitation became. One of the Palestinian participants did not like this and said angrily,

"I feel as though you are putting me in a jail!" Our way of talking had replicated, in microcosm, part of the dynamic we were try-ing to change.

Tough problems can only be solved if people talk openly, and in many situations this takes real courage. But this is not enough. The next step, listening openly, is even harder.

Listening

PART III

Openness

*I*F TALKING OPENLY means being willing to expose to others what is inside of us, then listening openly means being willing to expose ourselves to something new from others.

I observed the power of this simple directional shift in Houston, Texas. I was working with a group of powerful and public-spirited businessmen. They had a high confidence in their ability to wisely guide the city into the future and a low confidence in government and politicians.

The businessmen were concerned that the younger generation of business leaders were not sufficiently enthusiastic about becoming responsible "city fathers" and that politicians would step into this vacuum and ruin the city. They organized a team that included younger and minority businesspeople and a few leaders of large nonprofit organizations to talk about the situation and decide what to do. They were reluctant, however, to broaden the membership of the team further to include politicians and community leaders. They were afraid that a more diverse group would be both more awkward to work with and unnecessary. Businesspeople had previously figured out amongst themselves what was best for the city, and they could continue to do so.

These businessmen were willing to listen to each other, to CEO role models, to experts, and to younger business leaders. But they did not want to listen to anybody else. I thought that they were being arrogant in not valuing the potential contributions of non-business people. And I was being arrogant in not valuing their ideas about how they should contribute to their city.

One of our workshops was held in a big suburban hotel. The conversation was bogging down as the team members repeated their by-now-familiar views. I was getting frustrated with how closed, insular, and un-self-critical their views were. Then one of my cofacilitators, poet Betty Sue Flowers, pointed out that a large, loud convention of tattooists was getting started in the ballroom across the hall. Men and women with tattoos on every visible surface of their body were sharing our bagels, coffee, and fruit platters. Tattoo artists were setting up exhibition booths with huge photos of their work. Boxes of tattooing paraphernalia were piling up in the lobby. Rock music was blaring.

Flowers had worked with Jaworski on his book *Synchronicity* and was highly alert to meaningful coincidences. She suggested that during our next break each of us should walk across the hall and conduct a short interview of one of the tattooed people and then report back on what we learned. We were all uncomfortable with doing this, but we agreed. These encounters turned out to be a magically opening exercise. Many of our group found their interviews enlightening and reassuring. They saw for the first time what it was like to be treated as an outsider in Houston. They discovered they had more in common with the outsiders than they had assumed. These encounters let the team glimpse a part of the Houston system that had been invisible to them.

(I, by contrast, found my interview unexpectedly frightening. The man I interviewed had a tattoo of Jesus, to cover up one which he preferred but which was too unpopular to show openly: a swastika. Opening up to other people and to what is going on in the system of which we are part is not always a comfortable or comforting experience.)

This listening exercise was a turning point in the work of the team. As they talked about the dynamics between themselves and the tattooists, they understood that the issue of inclusion was central not only to how the city would develop but especially to how it would be led. By the end of the project, after several more meetings, they had concluded that the business community could no longer be led by a small number of white male CEOs of large companies. They decided that their core tasks had to be to "widen the circle" and "deepen the bench" of business leaders to include more women, minorities, and leaders of small companies, and to place greater emphasis on cooperating with politicians, city officials, and community leaders. The team went on to sponsor a series of ambitious initiatives to shape the future of Houston in this way.

To solve a complex problem, we have to immerse ourselves in and open up to its full complexity. Dynamic complexity requires us to talk not just with experts close to us, but also with people on the periphery. Generative complexity requires that we talk not only about options that worked in the past, but also about ones that are emerging now. And social complexity requires us to talk not just with people who see things the same way we do, but especially with those who see things differently, even those we don't like. We must stretch way beyond our comfort zone.

Looking back to my time as a student, it was absurdly closed of me to think that I could understand or influence the Brazilian energy situation without ever having been to Brazil or talked with a Brazilian. It was also absurd that in two years at PG&E, I never once had a meeting outside the PG&E building. Marvin Weisbord and Sandra Janoff, pioneers of the Future Search method of multi-stakeholder dialogue-and-action, argue that such stretching is essential: "Peer-only events . . . have little effect on the larger system. So our guiding principle, when we make out a Future Search invitation list, is: we want the 'whole system' in the room, meaning a larger system than usual."

One reason the Destino Colombia project had been less influential than it could have been is that the organizers decided to exclude any representatives of the administration of then-President Ernesto Samper, because his election campaign had been partly financed by drug traffickers. Manuel Jose Carvajal, the project's convenor, said to me afterwards that he thought this attempt to be "antiseptic" had been counterproductive, because as a result, the Samper government had resolutely ignored the team's ideas and its seminal work in constructing cross-boundary relationships. I talked about this with Max Hernandez, a Peruvian psychoanalyst and political activist. "Such a desire to be completely clean," he said, "is like an obsessive-compulsive disorder, where the patient is always washing his hands. It is not healthy to try to keep yourself away from everything unclean in the world."

Then Hernandez told me a story about one of his own experiences in Peru with cross-boundary dialogue. At one workshop, a businessman and a trade unionist left the meeting room and went for a long walk. Afterwards, the trade unionist told Hernandez: "I learned that this man's dreams are not my dreams. But nor are they my nightmares." "You have to remember," Hernandez told me, "that deep, dangerous conflict isn't usually the result of your rational argument versus my rational argument. It's the result of your rational argument hitting my blind spot, and vice versa. Listening openly helps us defuse this dynamic."

Norwegian professor Torkel Opsahl also understood the vital importance of open listening. During 1992 and 1993, he chaired a groundbreaking commission in Northern Ireland, called "A Citizen's Inquiry." The commission took written and oral submissions on the conflict from a wide range of community and political groups. When someone charged Opsahl with "talking with the Irish Republican Army," he replied, "I am not talking with the IRA. I am listening to the IRA."

Quaker peace activist Gene Knudsen Hoffman puts this imperative clearly:

We peace people have always listened to the oppressed and disenfranchised. That's very important. One of the new steps I think we should take is to listen to those we consider "the enemy" with the same openness, non-judgment, and compassion we listen to those with whom our sympathies lie. Everyone has a partial truth, and we must listen, discern, and acknowledge this partial truth in everyone—particularly those with whom we disagree.

Open listening is the basis for all creativity—in business and engineering as much as in politics. John Elter was the Xerox vice-president and chief engineer who led the innovation program that created the company's radical "Zero-to-Landfill" environmental vision and its Document Center products (which have brought in $40 billion of revenues). I once asked him what role he thought open listening played in the nuts-and-bolts creativity of new product development. "It is everything," he answered. "The challenges of product development are not about products. They are about interpersonal relations: power, trust, alignment. My team worked hard to learn how to listen, without judging, to what the other person was trying to say—really to be there. If we listen in the normal closed way, for what is right and what is wrong, then we won't be able to hear what is possible: what might be but is not yet. We won't be able to create anything new."

Reflectiveness

*T*HE SOUTH AFRICAN apartheid system was based on separating people—where they could live, study, work, and play—according to their race. People who challenged the system were banned from speaking in public, jailed, exiled, or assassinated. It was therefore not surprising that the members of the Mont Fleur team, coming from all races and political histories, some only recently released from jail or returned from exile, arrived at their first workshop in 1991 with radically different and strongly held views.

Given this background, the most extraordinary characteristic of the Mont Fleur process was the relaxed openness of the conversation. The team members not only spoke openly but, over the course of the meetings, changed what they said. They stretched more than the Basques, Paraguayans, and Canadians. This contrast allowed me to begin to answer the second question that I had been left with at the conclusion of Mont Fleur: How can we solve tough problems peacefully?

The members of the Mont Fleur team had listened, not only openly, but also reflectively. When they listened, they were not just reloading their old tapes. They were receptive to new ideas. More than that, they were willing to be influenced and changed. They held their ideas lightly; they noticed and questioned their own thinking; they separated themselves from their ideas ("I am not my ideas, and so you and I can reject them without rejecting me"). They "suspended" their ideas, as if on strings from the ceiling, and walked around and looked at these ideas from different perspectives.

What helped the team listen reflectively? Their personal qualities, their backgrounds in negotiating and in running democratic organizations, the historical turning point they faced, and the scenario methodology. Over and over, in those years, Nelson Mandela was modeling outstanding self-reflectiveness. He once said, "It was a tragedy to lose the best days of your life, but you learned a lot. You had time to think—to stand away from yourself, to look at yourself from a distance, to see the contradictions in yourself."

South Africa was in a moment of high generative complexity. The de Klerk government had suddenly taken down the walls, and South Africans knew that they had a once-in-a-lifetime opportunity to approach their problems in a new way. They realized that the old rules did not apply and that they had to be open in order to create new ones. In 2000 a team of researchers from the Massachusetts Institute of Technology and SoL (the Society for Organizational Learning) conducted interviews with members of the Mont Fleur team. One of these interviews was with Trevor Manuel, who said, "There was a high degree of flux at that time. That was a real strength. There was no paradigm, there was no precedent, and there was nothing; we had to *carve* it, and so perhaps we were more willing to listen."

The scenario exercise also encouraged openness and reflectiveness. The scenarios were what-if stories to play with, not predictions or proposals to sell. They emphasized multiple views about what might happen, rather than a single story about what would or should happen. They dealt with dynamic complexity because they addressed the whole situation in terms of causes and effects; with generative complexity because they addressed ways the future might be different from the past; and with social complexity because they created space not just for one "official future," but for many perspectives. Above all, they articulated links between the choices that the team members and their fellow citizens would make and the way in which the future would unfold.

In his interview, Howard Gabriels, from the left-wing black National Union of Mineworkers, remembered the sudden, confusing opening that occurred during the team's first brainstorming exercise:

> The first frightening thing was to look into the future without blinkers on. It was quite scary. . . . In the first workshop of the project we came up with 30 stories. At the time there was a euphoria about the future of the country, yet a lot of those stories were like "tomorrow morning you will open the newspaper and read that Nelson Mandela was assassinated," and what happened after that. Thinking about the future in that way was extremely frightening. All of a sudden you are no longer in your comfort zone. You are looking into the future and you begin to argue the capitalist case and the free market case and the social democracy case. Suddenly the capitalist starts arguing the communist case. And all those given paradigms begin to fall away. Those people that I thought were quite conservative were articulating very radical futures. . . . It was actually quite frightening in that one did not have the common base of a [shared political] manifesto, like your bible, that you could lean on.

When the members of the team listened reflectively, they were open not only to new ideas about the problem "out there," but also to new ideas about themselves. Johann Liebenberg was a white executive of the Chamber of Mines. Mining was South Africa's most important industry and the heart of its whites-only capitalism, with its operations deeply embedded in the apartheid system. On the left-dominated team, Liebenberg therefore represented the arch-establishment. His interview with the SoL researchers showed his and his teammates' extraordinary and exhilarating listening:

The team was a damn good team, a very diverse team of whites, blacks, Asians, coloreds, rich, poor, community workers, trade unionists, a really interesting mix. We would work together and play together . . . You go for a long walk after the day's work with Tito Mboweni on a mountain path and you just talk. Tito was the last sort of person I would have talked to a year before that. Very articulate, very bright; we did not meet blacks like that normally. I don't know where they were all buried but they were there. The only other blacks of that caliber that I had met were the trade unionists sitting opposite me in adversarial roles. This was new for me, especially how open-minded they were. These were not people who simply said: "Look, this is how it is going to be when we take over one day." They were prepared to say: "Hey, how *would* it be? Let's discuss it." But their pictures of the future and ours were not the same, and here was an opportunity, spread over a fairly lengthy period of time, for actually learning how other people think.

During one of the Mont Fleur workshops, Liebenberg was recording on a flipchart while Mosebyane Malatsi of the radical black Pan Africanist Congress—unofficial slogan: "One Settler [White Person], One Bullet"—was speaking. Liebenberg was calmly summarizing what Malatsi was saying: "Let me see if I've got this right. 'The illegitimate, racist regime in Pretoria . . .'" Liebenberg was able to hear and actually to articulate the inflammatory perspective of his opponent.

Liebenberg became friends with Gabriels, who had been his adversary throughout acrimonious and violent mining industry negotiations and strikes. Gabriels described how each man came to see the situation from the other's perspectives:

> In 1987 we took 340,000 workers out on strike. Fifteen workers were killed and more than 300 workers got terribly injured, and when I say injured, I do not only mean little

scratches. He was the enemy and here I was sitting with this guy in the room when those bruises are still raw. I think that Mont Fleur allowed him to see the world from my point of view and it allowed me to see the world from his point of view.

One of Liebenberg's comments illustrates how the team became able not only to see their situation from the perspective of others, but also to understand their own role in creating the situation:

> Look, I suppose that subconsciously we were all aware that what was being done to our brothers and sisters in this country was wrong. People were not being treated with dignity but . . . somebody else was doing it. *I* was treating people with dignity. But I was not doing anything to get my brothers to treat their brothers with dignity. So it was like the Germans in the Second World War. They saw nothing. Heard nothing. Nothing. That was the Gestapo that was doing it, not me.

To create new realities, we have to listen reflectively. It is not enough to be able to hear clearly the chorus of other voices; we must also hear the contribution of our own voice. It is not enough to be able to see others in the picture of what is going on; we must also see what we ourselves are doing. It is not enough to be observers of the problem situation; we must also recognize ourselves as actors who influence the outcome.

Bill Torbert of Boston College once said to me that the 1960s slogan "If you're not part of the solution, you're part of the problem" actually misses the most important point about effecting change. The slogan should be, he said, "If you're not part of the problem, you can't be part of the solution." If we cannot see how what we are doing or not doing is contributing to things being the way that they are, then logically we have no basis at all, zero leverage, for changing the way things are—except from the outside, by persuasion or force.

Reflectiveness is challenging in three ways. Philosophically, we are accustomed to believing that there is a world "out there" that exists apart from us and that we can see and manipulate objectively. But modern cognitive science teaches us that "cognition is not a representation of an independent, pregiven world, but rather a bringing forth of a world. What is brought forth by a particular organism in the process of living is not *the* world but *a* world, one that is always dependent on the organism . . ." Psychologically, we defend ourselves by focusing our attention first on what *others* are doing that is creating the problem situation. The shock I got from my Bastyr University T Group training was from seeing my own contribution—often unintentional—to creating the reality that was unfolding in the group. And politically, Torbert's axiom means that we can never help address a problem situation from a comfortable position of uninvolved innocence. If we want to help, we must first understand and acknowledge our role—by commission or omission—in creating the situation.

Avner Haramati is a psychologist and one of the leaders of an Israeli voluntary organization called Besod Siach, which in Hebrew means "the enigma of dialogue" and which comes from a Jewish prayer that refers to quiet communication among the angels. He told me about his experience working with groups in conflict and the central role of reflectiveness. "One key dynamic in any dialogue," he said, "is each party's monologue: the conversation each party is having among themselves. Once we organized a dialogue among leaders from the Israeli left, the settlers, and the ultra-orthodox. After the meeting ended, I got a lift back home in the car of the ultra-orthodox group. *That* conversation was much more lively and revealing than the conversation in the meeting had been. The big impact of the dialogue on them was that they got an alternative, challenging perspective on themselves and on their own policies."

In 1995, two years after I had left Shell, the company faced two serious crises in its relationships with external stakeholders. In both the case of the execution of Ken Saro-Wiwa, an anti-Shell activist, by the government of Nigeria, and the case of the planned dumping of the Brent Spar oil platform in the North Sea, the company dangerously misjudged what governments, non-governmental organizations, and the public expected of it, and so came close to losing its social "license to operate." Eventually Shell responded by engaging with these stakeholders and by making changes in its business practices, including incorporating human rights and environmental reviews into all project decisions. What I found significant is that the scenarios we had written in previous years had been insufficient to motivate the company's managers to effect these changes in their practices. Nor were they strongly motivated by the public criticism or boycotts as such; like managers of any large institution, they were used to being attacked. Their strongest motivation came from the self-reflective shock of seeing how much the perception that others had of them differed from their self-perception. Gary Steel, a senior manager, said, "As the public reacted against Shell after [Nigeria and Brent Spar], the company became an uncomfortable, disappointed, disenfranchised, negative place to work. It got to the point where at dinner parties, some of us were reluctant to say we worked for Shell."

The Mont Fleur team contributed to creating a new reality in South Africa because they were able to see themselves, reflectively and self-critically, as actors in the unfolding national drama. They understood that South Africa would change only if they themselves changed. If we want to change the systems we are part of—our countries, communities, organizations, and families—we must also see and change ourselves.

Empathy

*W*HEN I DID MY SCENARIO WORK at Shell and Mont Fleur, I believed that the key to solving complex problems was for people to listen openly and reflectively enough to change their thinking. Then I discovered that I was missing something.

I was leading a workshop in South Africa for the University of the North, a rural, apartheid-era institution with a history of conflict between radical black students and conservative white faculty and administration. The workshop included 100 students, faculty, and administrators. My fellow facilitator was a renowned black community organizer and political leader named Ishmael Mkhabela.

A few hours into the workshop, a shouting match broke out between the students and the staff. One year earlier, a student had been killed, and now the student leaders in the workshop were demanding a moment of silence in memory of their "martyr." The faculty did not want to celebrate a "troublemaker." The temperature in the room was rising, and my attempts to get everyone to be reasonable and cool down weren't working. I knew that I was stuck but did not know what to do, and I started to panic. Then Mkhabela calmly stepped forward to rescue me. "I suggest a moment of silence," he said, "both for this student and for all the others, students and staff, who have been hurt in this conflict . . . and for those who will come after us, for whom we are doing this work. Let us close our eyes . . ." The room fell silent and the fight dissolved.

That evening all the participants got together for a boisterous barbecue that spilled out of the hotel lobby and onto the lawn. I was circulating through the group, drink in hand, talking with the leaders, trying to understand what was going on and what we needed to do in the workshop the next day. I noticed with irritation that Mkhabela was spending the whole time sitting at a small table in the corner talking with one student. At the end of the evening we were walking back to our room, and I asked him what the hell he'd been doing, and why he had not been focusing on the workshop we had been hired to lead. His answer taught me what I had been missing. "Obviously, Adam," he said, "coming from the corporate world, you don't know much about grassroots organizing. This student, like a lot of young activists, has the terrible habit of speaking from his political party's 'we' and spouting their party line. I have just spent four hours with him, trying to connect to, and help him connect to, his authentic 'I.' The Black Consciousness movement taught us to examine the ways in which our mental attitudes contribute to our own oppression. I needed to help this student heighten his consciousness. This conversation was a real 'one-on-one': I talked with him heart to heart about what matters to him and what matters to me. Now tomorrow there will be two of us. This is how we have always done our organizing work in South Africa, and how we have succeeded in changing things: one person at a time."

Mkhabela's community-organizing approach to leading workshops and effecting change did not work from the outside and the top, but from the inside and the bottom. He did not spend the evening, as I had, talking superficially to many people, but deeply with one. He did not focus only on ideas but also on feelings and values and intentions. He did not tell the student what to do, but listened to how he thought and what mattered to him, heart to heart.

During the first months I lived in South Africa, I kept making a particular social gaffe. I would be walking on the street, trying to find an address, and I would stop someone and say, trying to be polite and get to the point, "Excuse me. Can you please tell me how to get to such-and-such a place?" Every time I did this, the person I had stopped would look at me in shock. Eventually, an older black man confronted me. He looked me straight in the eye and said, "Hello! How are you!?"

When I told this story to Dorothy, she explained that most South Africans consider it rude to approach someone and immediately launch into business. First you must greet them and ask after their well-being and the well-being of their family. In Zulu, the conventional greeting is "Sawu bona," which means "I see you." We cannot interact properly with others unless we see them as fellow humans.

Then I got the opportunity to learn more about this dynamic. I started working with a brilliant South African consultant named Louis van der Merwe. He taught me that the job of a facilitator is to help the participants speak up, listen up, and bring all of their personal resources to the work at hand. Our job is not to direct or control the participants. He also taught me that even though we were remaining neutral with respect to the substance of the participants' work, our process was not neutral: it embodied values of openness, inclusion, and collaboration. But van der Merwe and I used to argue a lot, and I came to feel increasingly discounted and unheard by him, which I found deeply distressing. I asked the advice of Betty Sue Flowers. "It is good for you that you have this experience," she said. "Most of the conflicts you are facilitating have their roots in some or all of the actors feeling unheard and unseen. Now you know what that feels like."

Joseph Jaworski is an exceptionally open listener. The core of his professional competence is his ability to listen with total presence, so that the boundary between him and the other person disappears. This quality of attention has a powerful impact on the person being listened to: the person feels heard and supported, becomes clearer about her or his own thoughts and feelings, and more centered and purposeful. The first time Jaworski and I conducted such a dialogue together, I was bored silly. As soon as we left the interviewee's office, I turned to Jaworski and asked him how he could pretend to be so deeply interested in the man's life and struggles. "But Adam," he replied, "I am *genuinely* interested in him! That's the whole point!"

We cannot develop creative solutions to complex human problems unless we can see, hear, open up to, and include the humanity of all the stakeholders and of ourselves. Creativity requires all of our selves: our thoughts, feelings, personalities, histories, desires, and spirits. It is not sufficient to listen rationally to inert facts and ideas; we also have to listen to people in a way that encourages them to realize their own potential and the potential in their situation. This kind of listening is not sympathy, participating in someone else's feeling from alongside them. It is empathy, participating from within them. This is the kind of listening that enables us not only to consider alternative existing ideas but to generate new ones.

This is not the kind of listening I was taught in my physics and economics courses. I needed to open up and to sense subjectively from the inside phenomena that were real but could not be seen objectively from the outside. Once I was a faculty member in a four-day, dialogic workshop organized by the Society for Organizational Learning and led by Peter Senge. During the whole week I was suffering from a terrible allergy and coughing all the time; so although I attended all the sessions and made a few presentations, I wasn't fully present. At the end of the week, we were all reflecting on what we had gotten out of the workshop. I was surprised to hear how moving and transformational the experience had been for almost everyone—I hadn't noticed anything going on at all. This very real intra-, inter-, and transpersonal phenomenon had been completely invisible to me because I, preoccupied with my illness, had remained outside the experience.

Maria Victoria Giraldo, a Spanish-English interpreter from the Destino Colombia workshops, is an outstandingly empathetic listener. As she interpreted different Spanish-speaking members of that team, she gave each person's words a distinctly different tone. When I spoke with her during the breaks, she always had significant insights into the underlying dynamics in the group. I asked her how she did her work, and she said that she imagined herself speaking from within the person she was interpreting. (I also asked her what her experience was of speaking from within the angry, violent members of the team. "Afterwards," she replied, "I cannot sleep.")

Otto Scharmer talked with me a lot about such distinctions in the location of the listener. He was developing a taxonomy of four different ways of listening. The first is "downloading," or listening *from within our own story,* but without being conscious that what we are saying and hearing is no more than a story. When we download, we are deaf to other stories; we only hear that which confirms our own story. This is the kind of nonlistening exhibited by fundamentalists, dictators, experts, and people who are arrogant or angry.

The second kind of listening is "debating." When we debate, we listen to each other and to ideas (including our own ideas) *from the outside,* objectively, like a judge in a debate or a courtroom.

When we are downloading or debating, we are merely exhibiting and reproducing already-existing ideas and realities. We are not producing anything new, and we are not being creative. These first two kinds of listening are therefore insufficient to create new social realities.

Scharmer calls the third kind of listening "reflective dialogue." We engage in such dialogue when we listen to ourselves reflectively and when we listen to others empathetically—listening *from the inside,* subjectively.

But Scharmer also referred to a fourth kind of listening, which he calls "generative dialogue." He said that in generative dialogue we listen not only from within ourselves or from within others, but *from the whole of the system.* But I needed to stretch much further before I could understand what it meant to listen from the whole.

Creating New Realities

PART IV

Cracking Through
the Egg Shell

I HAD THE OPPORTUNITY to witness generative dialogue in the shambles of Argentina. In
December 2001, after three years of deepening recession and rising unemployment, Argentines marched, rioted, looted, and
brought down their elected government. The country had five
presidents in two weeks. When I started making trips to
Argentina in the months that followed, things were going from
bad to worse: the currency crashed, the country defaulted, banks
closed, professionals emigrated. Suddenly, in a country that had
had the highest standard of living in Latin America, one-half of
the population was living in poverty, one-quarter in destitution,
and children were dying of hunger.

Almost nobody believed that Argentines could solve their own
problems. Month after month, political leaders failed to agree on
an emergency reform program. Politicians hesitated to walk in
the streets because people so despised them. One popular slogan
was "They Must All Go!" International commentators wrote the
country off. The conventional wisdom among both locals and
foreigners was that Argentines were too closed, partisan, con-
frontational, and egotistical to sit down together and agree on
what to do. I heard many quips: "The best business in the world
is to buy Argentines for what they're worth and sell them for what
they think they're worth." "In Argentina, consensus means that

you agree with me." I was told over and over: "Argentines are incapable of dialogue." The only solutions I heard people mention were ones imposed from outside or above: a new, strong, dynamic president—like Peron; an economic regime imposed by the International Monetary Fund; a military government.

In January 2002, at the height of this fatalism and messianism, some Argentines decided to try a new, more open approach. A small group of citizens, with the support of the government, the Catholic Church, and the United Nations Development Programme, launched a process they called "Argentine Dialogue." They brought together hundreds of leaders from all parts of society in a series of roundtables, to talk about the crisis, to make proposals, and to act.

One of these roundtables focused on the issue of justice. Argentina's judicial system was so inefficient, inaccessible, politicized, and corrupt that in many cases disputes couldn't be resolved, nor contracts or laws enforced, nor human rights abuses contested. The problems in the justice system exemplified and were a central part of the accumulated problems in the larger Argentine system. Solutions for justice were critical to long-term solutions for the country.

Activists had been fighting for decades to reform the system, but had never been able to get agreement among a critical mass of the system's leaders. Now six of these activists thought that the Argentine Dialogue provided them with an opportunity. "The crisis in our country is so severe," one of them, Santiago Gallichio, said to me, "that people are willing to try to do things in a different way. We are in an open moment."

When these activists invited me to work with them, I thought carefully about the stance I should take in doing this work. I decided to hold a position of unwavering optimism: to believe in the capacity of Argentines to resolve their problems through "the miraculous option." I gave an interview to *La Nación*, the country's newspaper of record: "The options for Argentina are violence or dialogue. You can wait for someone to impose a solution from on high, or you can sit together and work through a solution yourselves."

In September 2002, we held a three-day workshop in a countryside hotel with fifty leaders of the justice system: judges, lawyers, citizens' rights advocates, government officials, court workers, businesspeople, law professors, legal journalists, politicians. Although many of them knew each other from previous formal encounters in courtrooms or classrooms, this workshop was organized differently. No papers were presented and no resolutions passed. Instead they talked, in small groups and in plenary, about the justice system, what it had inherited from its past, what was certain and uncertain about its future, their vision of the future they wanted, and what points of leverage would shift the system towards that vision.

After dinner on the second day, the team members sat in a circle of comfortable chairs. The meeting room was now lit with candles and stocked with wine and whisky. One of my cofacilitators, Paraguayan Jorge Talavera, invited each person to tell a personal story that might shed light on why they had chosen to participate in this work. We heard twenty stories, all of them from the heart. In four of the first stories, the storyteller or someone in their family had almost died—choking, cancer, a coma—and then miraculously had come back to life. Many of the stories dealt with terrible injustices suffered by the storyteller or a member of their family and how they had vowed to fight for a better system of justice. Two men sitting next to one another spoke of fathers imprisoned for political reasons—by opposing political factions. Finally, one man, who all day had been pacing and fidgeting on the edge of the group, cleared his throat and launched into a long love poem. It was a stunning conclusion to a moving evening.

On the final morning of the workshop, the group's conversations and ideas came together quickly. Team members announced initiatives that they wanted to spearhead, and groups formed around these leaders to make plans. In the months after the workshop, they executed these plans, convened again and made new plans, and executed these as well. They were on their way towards creating a new reality.

Over the course of these three days, a diverse and fragmented group of fifty leaders who were part of a complex, stuck problem made dramatic progress in unsticking it. They all arrived with their own perspectives and projects, disconnected and in many cases at odds with those of others. Many of them were despairing and resigned to a future that was spiraling downwards. By the time they left, they had built a broad and aligned coalition for change, with new and reoriented projects and teams, grounded in a shared sense of their situation and what they needed to do about it. Most of them left hopeful and engaged in building the future up again. In reclaiming and thereby shifting the future of the justice system, they were contributing to shifting the future of the country.

I was impressed with what the group accomplished and with the intelligence and openheartedness with which they accomplished it. I did not say very much during the workshop—Talavera and a team of Argentine facilitators led most of the sessions —and I enjoyed sitting and listening and appreciating the beauty of the unfolding. The Mont Fleur meetings had probably also been characterized by such a beautiful, generative unfolding, but at the time I hadn't been experienced or open enough to see it. In Argentina, I was committed to helping the group make progress in their work, and yet able to be present and relaxed through the meeting's usual ups and downs.

National leaders who were not at the workshop noticed that this particular approach to reforming the justice system had accomplished something different and important, which offered encouragement and lessons for other dialogic reform efforts. The day after the workshop, the lead editorial in *La Nación* proclaimed:

When on January 14, 2002, citizens from different socio-economic, political, and ideological backgrounds sat at the Argentine Dialogue table, many regarded this attempt with that unhealthy skepticism of those that believe that the Argentines have an innate and unredeemable lack of capacity.... Despite all this, the willingness of citizens to dialogue kept confidence alive and ... showed that it was possible to build consensus, hardly perceptible at some sectoral tables but oozing with hope in the case of the one focusing on the reform of the justice system. An experiment never before tried in our country has just started up that will show others willing to dialogue how to do so.

This success was achieved through a shift in the way the team members talked and listened. They came to the meeting prepared—as befitted a group of lawyers and judges—to make their arguments and to judge the arguments of others. At the beginning they were nervous and cautious, not so much listening as waiting for their turn to pontificate, to deliver their official, already-thought-through speeches. As they relaxed and got caught up in the excitement of the work and the engaging process, they started listening more openly and speaking more spontaneously and frankly.

In the closing session of the meeting, one team member reflected on what had happened:

A physical feeling that we often have here in Argentina is that we are submerged under water like divers. Each one of us has our own idea, an idea which we have to convey through gestures, and the others don't quite understand what the idea is. I think that this meeting surfaced those ideas like floating blocks, towards which the divers swam up. When we reached the surface, we took off our divers' suits, and started to voice our ideas and to turn them into agreements.

On the final morning, the team made their action plans quickly and fluidly, completing each other's sentences. During the session of final comments, they spoke as one. "We overcame the 'Tango Effect,'" one judge said in the closing session, "that dramatic, nostalgic, fatalistic Argentine way of saying, 'We cannot make it.'"

Three days of dialogue did not, of course, accomplish the reform of the justice system. What it did was shift an old, degenerating system suffering from the apartheid syndrome onto a new, more open, regenerating path—as had been foreshadowed in the second evening's stories of death and resurrection. One team member said we were engaged in a process of "reforestation." We were planting seedlings of a new ecology, which now needed protecting and nurturing. With time, these seedlings could replace the old ecology.

The workshop participants demonstrated that, contrary to conventional wisdom, Argentines are capable of dialogue and of working together. Underneath the shift in the way they talked and listened was a shift in the way they positioned themselves in relation to the judicial system. At the beginning they were observers of the system, standing outside of it, complaining and blaming others—the government, the Supreme Court, each other—for its terrible state. By the end they were committed, creative actors. One of them said in the closing session:

> I am pleased that somehow I am doing something so that the youth, the capable people, do not leave my country. When I get back home I can tell my children, "Look, it is possible, you just have to sit down and work, each from your own place, in order to rebuild our country." Once again we feel proud to say, "I am staying because I am sure that it is going to be the best thing I can do for my future and that of my community."

This key shift from observer to actor, from reactor to creator, was particularly meaningful against the backdrop of Argentine messianism. Rather than watch and wait and pray for a new president or boss or benefactor who would create a better future for them, they chose to start the work themselves. At the end of 2002, Christina Calvo, one of the Catholic Church's lay leaders of the Argentine Dialogue, made this same point with a religious image. She sent out a Christmas card with this message:

> I remember that during the height of the crisis early in December 2001, many of us were upset that our beautiful Christmas was being ruined. But Jesus did not change the time in which he was called upon to be born. In the middle of persecutions, inequalities, and empires, his life marked the beginning of a new epoch. May we have the force to imitate him!

A problem that is generatively complex cannot be solved with a prepackaged solution from the past. A solution has to be worked out as the situation unfolds, through a creative, emergent, generative process. This Argentine workshop was part of such a process: it produced results that were not anticipated or proposed at the outset.

The team achieved this generativity through a conversation that went through three phases. First, it diverged, when they raised a lot of different ideas about what was going on in the justice system. Then it emerged, when they developed new ideas and also a sense of what this all meant and what they had to do. And then it converged, when they decided on their initiatives and plans.

The team found the middle, emerging phase unfamiliar and frustrating. As lawyers and judges, they were used to linear problem-solving processes, with ideas presented, debated, and judged in a preset sequence. But I once explained these phases to a Hollywood screenwriter, and he responded, "I recognize that. When a group of us are working on a script, tossing ideas around, what you call 'emerging' is what we call 'cooking.' New ideas just come up and you don't know who said them or where they came from."

The point at which the conversation turned, and the team's sense of what they had to do emerged, occurred during the evening storytelling session. The participants' talking and listening opened up dramatically. Santiago Gallichio, flabbergasted, described the evening by saying: "The thin shell of the egg broke and everything spilled out!" The boundary that separates us from others is thin, and simple—although not always easy—to crack through.

That evening the participants listened intently, with empathy and wonder, and they spoke surprisingly personally and emotionally. They listened with and spoke from their hearts. Their stories were the window through which they could see two critical phenomena: each other as fellow humans and actors and, beyond the individuals, what was emerging in the situation as a whole and what it demanded of them. Here were what Scharmer had called reflective and generative dialogue.

The stories enabled the participants to understand their individual and group roles as part of the problem and what they needed to do to be part of the solution. These understandings can occur through any kind of open conversation, but they often occur through personal storytelling. When people choose to tell a personal story in such a group, they are revealing something of themselves. They are sharing what matters to them about this problem. Furthermore, because (in Carl Rogers' paradoxical phrase) "what is most personal is most universal," these stories also illuminate the source of the group's shared commitment.

The point at which a team achieves such a creative "click" can, in the context of a crisis like Argentina's, be dramatic. But in more ordinary circumstances, it can be subtle. I have seen this same click in a group of Canadian civil servants, as they remembered the value of public service that had drawn them to join the government in the first place. I have seen it in a group of American accountants, as they remembered the vital role their profession was supposed to play in ensuring the integrity of financial markets. The common theme in all of these cases is that the participants were able to sense (or remember) what the larger purpose was for their work and why it mattered to them individually and as a group—the sources of their shared commitment.

In order to solve tough problems, we need more than shared new ideas. We also need shared commitment. We need a sense of the whole and what it demands of us.

One year later, at the end of 2003, I went to Argentina again. The economic, political, and social state of the country was recovering. This was due in part to the work of the Argentine Dialogue. Participants had not only brokered specific agreements to address the crisis—for example, an emergency subsidy for impoverished families—but also helped to de-escalate the conflict through the safe spaces it opened up for multi-stakeholder conversations.

I attended a meeting of the members of the justice dialogue team. They were reviewing what had happened in the judicial system in the fifteen months since our first workshop. They were delighted and also flummoxed. The government was in the process of implementing a sweeping program of judicial reform (including replacing most members of the Supreme Court) that was completely in line with the vision that the team had articulated at that first workshop. And yet the team couldn't make out, looking back over the intervening months, the exact cause and effect between the workshop and the current reforms. Clearly they had influenced that change in the system—but they had not controlled it. They had provided visible leadership of the judicial reform effort and, at the same time, had simply been a small manifestation of their time's much larger reform movement.

I talked this over with Ramón Brenna, a thoughtful member of the team who had been working on judicial reform for decades. "This group is used to *forcing* change," he said. "But in this case we *generated* change. We are struggling to understand what that means."

Later I spoke about this distinction at length with my colleague Alain Wouters, with whom I had worked at Shell. He has a solid theoretical and practical understanding of how change occurs in complex systems. While I had been working in Argentina, he had been doing similar, high-stakes, multi-stakeholder work in Burundi. "I think," he said, "that 'solving tough problems' doesn't accurately describe what we and these teams are doing. When we talk about 'solving a problem,' we imply that we stand apart from the problem and can study it objectively and control it mechanically, with cause producing effect, as we would with a broken-down car. But this isn't a good model of our increasingly complex and interdependent and rapidly changing world. There is not 'a' problem out there that we can react to and fix. There is a 'problem situation' of which each of us is a part, the way an organ is part of a body. We can't see the situation objectively: we can just appreciate it subjectively. We affect the situation and it affects us. The best we can do is to engage with it from multiple perspectives, and try, in action-learning mode, to improve it. It's more like unfolding a marriage than it is like fixing a car.

"But this way of understanding the world," he continued, "has serious consequences. If we admit that we are part of co-creating the way things are, then we are also co-responsible for the way things are. This is the moral and political challenge implicit in the comment Torbert made to you, that 'if you're not part of the problem, you can't be part of the solution.' This was the daunting realization that we both had ten years ago in Shell, when we sensed the limitation of writing scenarios of the future as if we and Shell had no impact on how the future would unfold.

"And this way of understanding the world has another implication that is even more deeply challenging. This world is too complex and interdependent and rapidly changing for us to be able to reason through everything that is going on. We can no longer rely only on *making sense* of the whole of what is going on: we also have to *sense* it. This requires us to access a deeper, nonrational, more ancient kind of knowing."

Closed Fist, Open Palm

THE WAY TO LISTEN is to stop talking. One reason we cannot hear what others are saying is that their voices are drowned out by our own internal voices. We keep reacting and projecting, judging and prejudging, anticipating and expecting, reloading and drifting off. The biggest challenge of listening is quieting down our internal chatter. When we succeed in doing so, we see the world anew.

Jaworski and I were helping a team from a European multinational company that was working to turn around the dismal sales performance of their oldest and biggest division. They had been studying the situation for months, interviewing colleagues, customers, competitors, and people in other industries. We met for a three-day workshop in a small inn in the French Pyrenees. We spent the first morning analyzing the overwhelming mass of interview material. Then we walked up a nearby mountain and spread out along a ridge with magnificent views of snow-capped peaks and rocky valleys. We spent the next sixteen hours there, each with our own tent, alone and silent, without cell phones or watches or books or paper. We had no problem-solving assignment. Our guide, meditation teacher John Milton, simply asked us to relax and be fully present with what was going on inside and around us.

For my first several hours on the ridge, I was not at all relaxed or present. My mind was buzzing and hopping about with thoughts and worries about the past and the future: what I wished I'd said, what I needed to remember to do. Then, as I sat looking out at the huge vista and then later at the night sky, this buzzing within my head subsided, the ideas and worries dropped away, and I felt myself opening up to something larger and more encompassing. Then the next morning, just before we were all to meet up and descend the mountain, a few new ideas popped into my mind, from nowhere, about what we had to do next.

We descended and then returned to our workshop. We did not talk much about what had happened to us during our silence. Yet our subsequent working sessions had a radically new character. Our conversations were unusually open, honest, fluid, purposeful, and generative. The team came to a new understanding of their business problem and then quickly and easily agreed on a set of initiatives to address it.

Yet this exceptionally productive three-day conversation included one full day of not talking at all. The impact of our quiet time was not so much on the quality of our talking. Nobody came down from the mountain with an epiphany. Its impact was on the quality of our listening. By relaxing and calming down, we became better able to listen to ourselves, to each other, and to the situation and what it demanded of us.

Economist Brian Arthur, from the Santa Fe Institute of Complexity Sciences, was a guest at this workshop. We had invited him to speak to us because of a provocative comment he had made to an interviewer from *Fast Company* magazine:

> For the big decisions in life, you need to reach a deeper region of consciousness. Making decisions then becomes not so much about "deciding" as about letting an inner wisdom emerge. We've been bamboozled into believing that cognition is rational—that our mind is a gigantic computer, or a blackboard on which we can reach a decision by calculating pluses and minuses. Recent research on cognition shows that our minds rarely make strictly logical

deductions. Instead, we rely on patterns—and on feelings associated with those patterns.

At the workshop, Arthur talked to us about the process of scientific innovation that he had observed in his own work and in that of his Nobel Prize–winning biologist and physicist colleagues. He said that good scientists solve everyday problems by "lowering onto a problem" a preexisting theory (downloading), and then using that theory to calculate a solution. But this approach does not work for creating breakthroughs. For this, great scientists "camp out beside a problem," studying it assiduously and waiting for an intuitive insight. In real innovation, the "click" does not come from working on and talking about a problem, but from stepping back, giving our unconscious some space to work, and listening for an answer. This is what we had done on the mountain.

On a smaller scale, I noticed this same phenomenon while working on this book. I was at my family's home beside the beach in Cape Town. I would be stuck trying to figure out how to express an idea, and I would quit and go for a five-minute swim in the sea. By the time I got back to my desk I would know what to write. The same thing happened when I was brushing my teeth before going to bed. As soon as I retreated from the problem, a solution came.

Miha Pogacnik is an exuberant Slovenian concert violinist and a wonderful teacher of listening. With a new group of students, he plays a short piece of music and then asks them what they heard. Invariably one of the students answers, "I liked it." Pogacnik insists: "I don't care whether you liked it or didn't like it! Tell me what you heard!" He wants to teach his students to hear and to notice differences in tempo, color, mood, and energy. Our biggest impediment to hearing is our impulse to talk rather than to listen, to make a judgment rather than an observation.

Kees van der Heijden emphasized the same point when he coached us on how to conduct interviews at Shell. He wanted us to hear precisely what the interviewee was saying and to write it down without filtering or distorting it, especially when it differed from our own thinking. Van der Heijden himself was a masterfully conscientious listener. I once conducted a series of interviews sitting side-by-side with him. Afterwards, when we reviewed our two sets of notes, I was astounded at how much I had failed to hear. My prejudices—my prejudgments—about what was important had distorted my ability to hear accurately what the interviewees were saying.

I am at my best as a leader and facilitator when I am relaxed and present to what is arising: when I am able to hear and help others to hear what is happening in and amongst and around us, and what I and we need to do. I fail as a leader when I am so preoccupied with what I want to make happen—to force to happen—that I miss what is actually happening.

In the summer of 2002, Betty Sue Flowers and I facilitated a small meeting of CEOs at the Aspen Institute in Colorado, on the social responsibility of business. In the aftermath of September 11 and Enron, the subject of trust and mutual understanding—between companies and their stakeholders, between leaders and followers, between the United States and Europe and the Arab world—figured prominently in our sessions. One afternoon, we drove to a beautiful valley and split up to take a one-hour solo, silent walk. Then we reconvened around a campfire to continue our conversation and to eat dinner. I was determined that in this session after our quiet walks in this uplifting setting, we would have our magical insight. The participants were relaxed, happy, and human. They had been inspired by their walks and were enjoying recounting what had come to them. But I was not satisfied. I sternly urged them to dig deeper.

Suddenly, the one Arab member of the group wildly interrupted our conversation by riding up to the campfire on a horse. He had met some men on his walk, and they had offered him a beer and let him ride one of their horses. "This is what my culture is like!" he said excitedly. My serious dialogue dissolved as the group erupted into delighted laughter. But I was so preoccupied with my disappointment at failing to manufacture magic that I was not present enough to recognize the magic that had come riding up into our group.

Harrison Owen is a pioneering facilitator who has developed a highly open and self-directed dialogue-and-action methodology called Open Space. We were corresponding about his and my approaches to process facilitation, and he wrote to me:

> I wonder whether you aren't working too hard to achieve something that can happen pretty much by itself. I certainly agree that open talking and open listening and the other elements you are paying attention to are critical, but how do we get these? Twenty years with Open Space has pretty well convinced me that all of these elements are naturally occurring phenomena which happen pretty much by themselves, if given the space. Lots of chaos, confusion, and conflict, to be sure—but I find that this unholy trinity has much to contribute.

If we want to help resolve complex problem situations, we have to get out of the way of situations that are resolving themselves.

By this time, my work on solving tough problems was focused comfortably on opening up my listening and helping others do the same. Then John Milton, the meditation and martial arts teacher who had guided the group in the Pyrenees, said something that brought me up short. All of a sudden, I realized that my focus was seriously unbalanced—that I was missing half of the story.

It was at the end of a Tai Chi lesson. Milton bowed to us with his hands held in a way I had never seen before. His right hand was curled into a fist and it was cupped by his left hand. Afterwards, I asked him what this meant. "This is an ancient mudra or sacred hand gesture," he said. "The right hand, in a loosely clenched fist, represents the yang, the masculine. In the classical Chinese text, *The I Ching, or Book of Changes,* it is called 'The Creative.' The left hand, which softly holds the right, represents the yin, the feminine, and is called 'The Receptive.'" Then he smiled at me. "The right hand represents open talking. The fist is not clenched tightly: you should be able to pull a pencil through it. It represents talking *with*, not talking *at*. And the left hand represents open listening."

Most of us need to work even harder on opening up our listening than on opening up our talking. But we can't solve tough problems through listening alone—just as we can't solve them through talking alone. If we want to create new realities, we need to listen and be, but we also need to talk and act. Open listening and open talking are yin and yang, two parts of the same whole, two movements in the same generative dance.

The Wound That
Wants to Be Whole

$\mathcal{I}$N GUATEMALA, I observed this generative dance in a beautiful and terrible context. Guatemala had, from 1960 to 1996, the longest-running and most brutal civil war in Latin America. Even the torture instructors hired from Argentina were appalled by what they witnessed. Out of a total population of 7 million, more than 200,000 people were "disappeared" (killed), and more than 1 million were forcibly displaced. The Guatemalan state was responsible for almost all of this violence, and they directed almost all of it against the country's indigenous people, the Mayans.

The official, internationally supported investigation of this period was the "Commission for Historical Clarification." Their report is appalling to read. It documents the use of terror, torture, kidnappings, child soldiers, a militarized police, arbitrary executions, rape, and semi-official death squads; the closing of political spaces, weakening of social organizations, and denial of justice; massacres and genocide. Guatemala exhibited the most extreme possible version of the apartheid syndrome.

In 1996, after ten years of negotiations, the government and the guerrillas signed a set of Peace Accords. Guatemalans started to sweep up the broken pieces and rebuild their lives and their country. With energy and creativity, they launched initiatives to repair the shattered society. Amidst the destruction, they started to seed a new, more open and hopeful future. Guatemala is a country of extremes and bright colors: the worst and best of humanity in one landscape.

One of these rebuilding initiatives was Visión Guatemala. It was inspired by Mont Fleur and intended to support the implementation of the Peace Accords. Its members were academics, business and nongovernmental organization leaders, former guerrillas and military officers, government officials, human rights activists, journalists, national and local politicians, clergy, trade unionists, and young people. I was awestruck by this team's talking and listening and by what, over the years that followed, they produced.

Their first workshop was held in 1998 at a hotel in the highlands, four hours from the capital, beside Lake Atitlán, in the shadow of the Toliman volcano. It started awkwardly and formally. The participants were deeply mistrustful of one another. Project director Elena Diez Pinto later recalled to researchers from the Society for Organizational Learning:

> When I arrived at the hotel for lunch before the start of the initial meeting, the first thing I noticed was that the indigenous people were sitting together. The military guys were sitting together. The human rights group was sitting together. I thought, "They are not going to speak to each other." In Guatemala, we have learned to be very polite. We are so polite that we say "Yes" but think "No." I was worried that we would be so polite that the real issues would never emerge.

After lunch, the team moved into the meeting room. They moved their chairs into a circle, and each person presented an object that for them symbolized the current reality of Guatemala. This exercise immediately plunged us into a bewildering panorama of perspectives: a cob of corn, a staple food, and the seeds for more food, out of which, according to Mayan legend, humanity was formed; several pieces of traditional woven clothing, made up of many bright colors of wool, representing the country's diverse ethnic groups; a stone, representing Mother Earth; a photo of someone's five-year-old daughter; two copies of the Peace Accords; a poster of Myrna Mack, an anthropologist who had been assassinated for conducting research on people displaced by the war.

The meeting continued in this vein, with a series of sessions aimed at uncovering the complex reality of Guatemala. Even a simple listening exercise—"After lunch, go for a one-hour walk outside with someone you haven't spoken with yet"—produced excitement and revelation. After decades of terror and fragmentation, the participants were delighted with the opportunity simply to talk openly with one another. One team member later commented on the surprise and impact of these interactions:

> We are unaware of the great richness in others. We do not see it. There is a lot, quite a lot, to learn from people who, frankly speaking, one would never have considered as possible sources of learning.

Another team member had this to say:

> The first round in the first session was extremely negative because we were all looking back to the events of recent years, which had left a deep imprint on us. A first moment full of pessimism was generated. Suddenly, a young man stood up and questioned our pessimism in a very direct manner. This moment marked the beginning of an important change, and we continually referred to it afterwards. That a young man would suddenly call us "old pessimists" was an important contribution.

After dinner on the second day, we gathered to tell stories. This session was riveting and moving. We heard many stories about the civil war. Businesswoman Helen Mack Chang was the sister of Myrna Mack, who in 1990 had been assassinated by the military in broad daylight. Helen told the story of how she had run, furious, from government office to government office trying to find out why her sister had been killed. In the workshop that evening, she addressed her story firmly and calmly to the man sitting next to her in the circle—the same army officer, from the feared G2 intelligence unit, who had been on duty that day and who had lied to her and told her that he knew nothing.

The next morning the plenary session was open for anyone to speak. Often, after having slept on the previous day's conversations, participants bring up new and significant matters. I was relaxed, present, open, and curious, listening for what might come up, not expecting anything in particular. A man named Ronalth Ochaeta said he had a story that he wanted to tell. Ochaeta was the director of the Guatemalan Archdiocesan Human Rights Office, which was documenting the atrocities of the civil war.

Ochaeta had gone to a Mayan village to witness the exhumation of a mass grave—one of many—from a massacre. When the earth had been removed, he noticed a number of small bones. He asked the forensics team if people had had their bones broken during the massacre. No, the grave contained the corpses of women who had been pregnant. The small bones belonged to their fetuses.

When Ochaeta finished telling his story, the team was completely silent. I had never heard a story like this. I was struck dumb. I had no idea what to say or do, so I said and did nothing. I looked around the circle and caught the eye of an old man, who simply nodded at me slowly. The silence lasted a long time, perhaps five minutes. Then it ended, and we took a break.

This silence had an enormous impact on the group. In interviews years later, many members of the team referred to it. In the words of one member:

The group gained the possibility of speaking frankly. Things could be said without upsetting the other party. I believe this helped to create a favorable atmosphere in which to express, if not the truth, certainly each person's truth. This, I believe, was finally achieved. In the end, and particularly after listening to Ochaeta's story, I understood and felt in my heart all that had happened. And there was a feeling that we must struggle to prevent this from happening again.

Another member put it this way:

That was one story, and there must be a thousand like it. What happened in this country was brutal . . . But we were aware of it! I was! I was a politician for a long time and this was one of the areas that I worked in. I was even threatened by the military on account of my political work. We suffered, but as opponents, as enemies, always from our particular point of view. As far as I am concerned, the workshops helped me understand this in its true human dimension. A tremendous brutality! I was aware of it but had not experienced it. It is one thing to know about something and keep it as statistical data, and another to actually feel it . . . And I think that all of us had to go through this process. I think that, after understanding this, everyone was committed to preventing it from happening again.

Another remembered the impact of the silence:

His testimony was sincere, calm and serene, without a trace of hate in his voice. This gave way to the moment of silence that, I would say, lasted at least one minute. It was horrible! A very moving experience for all . . . If you ask any of us, we would say that this moment was like a large communion. No one dared break the silence.

Another also emphasized the power of silence:

> Silence has an incredible capacity to bond. You simply
> remain silent and nobody has to say anything. We're there,
> all of us together.

At the end of that session, I made what was for me an unchar-
acteristic comment: "I felt there was spirit in the room." Afterwards, a young Mayan man came up to me: "Why were you
surprised that there was a spirit in the room? Don't you know
that today is our Day of the Spirits?" I never understood exactly
what he meant, except that whatever had happened during those
five minutes was more familiar to him than it was to me.

A second workshop was held two months after the first, in
which the team continued with their work of uncovering the reality of Guatemala. Historians offered alternative stories of
Guatemala's recent past. A panel of businessmen and economists
explained the challenges of national development in the context
of globalizing markets. Three Mayan scholars talked about
indigenous cosmology and culture. This session was significant
because the country's Ladino (white or mestizo) minority had
ignored, discriminated against, and killed people in the Mayan
majority. Like most oppressed people, the Mayans were unseen,
and now they were being seen.

In one session, the team engaged in a particularly difficult dialogue about the findings of the Commission for Historical Clarification. Julio Balconi, a retired army general, was struggling to
get the others to understand how, during the war, he had done
what he thought he had to do to defend the country. This was a
perspective that many members of the team found hard to hear.
Raquel Zelaya, the cabinet secretary of peace, charged with over-
seeing the implementation of the Peace Accords, leaned over and
said to him gently, with great empathy, "I know that nobody
enrolls in the military academy in order to learn how to massacre
women and children."

Out of these broad and deep explorations of Guatemala's past and present, the team constructed a set of scenarios of what might happen in the future. They also constructed a vision of the future that they wanted to create—not pulled out of thin air but rooted in their now broader and deeper understanding of the reality of the system. They called their vision *The Flight of the Fireflies* because it described a social system not focused on the light of one messianic leader, but constructed and illuminated by the diverse contributions of everyone, including the Mayans. Part of this vision was that after so many years of nightmarish division and repression, Guatemalans would "recover their capacity to dream together." One participant put it this way:

> Very few people have the privilege of collective dreaming, which is intoxicating. The fact that you can sit and begin to converge on a series of issues in which you are not just making it up, but you are actually trying to root it in reality . . . and also to grasp it up with all of your strength, so that you can in fact envision what you sense. That sensation is very powerful.

The scenarios and vision were only the beginning. They were a means for the team to grasp the whole of their situation and what they needed to do about it. In the words of a university president:

> What place to assign to the construction of scenarios as such? It is good that they were made, but that was not necessarily what was most important. The story of the scenarios is like the story anthropologist Bronislaw Malinowsky tells of a system he discovered in some South Sea islands. He found that an extremely sophisticated mechanism exists by which people from some islands travel to others and make exchanges of shells. From the point of view of economic logic, this makes no sense at all: to risk lives in very long

voyages to exchange sea shells. But in the end he discovers that the shells are the great pretext to do another whole bunch of things that are the ones that really matter. I believe that the scenarios are the shells of Visión Guatemala. They were the great pretext to do what we needed to do.

Lars Franklin, the United Nations Development Programme's representative in Guatemala, said that Visión Guatemala could best be understood by looking at the many seeds the project planted and nurtured. These seeds included influencing the platforms of three of the major political parties; participating in the vital commissions on Historical Clarification, the monitoring of the Peace Accords, and a new Fiscal Pact; and contributing to a constitutional amendment campaign, a national antipoverty program, several municipal development strategies, and the reform of both primary school and university curricula. "Visión Guatemala is," one team member said, "a parable of the best that can happen in this country."

A government member of Visión Guatemala was reflective:

> I don't know how much of what has been happening later in Guatemala has to do with Visión Guatemala . . . It is difficult to assess. Visión Guatemala is almost like the Apostles to whom Christ said: take up your cross and follow me. It hasn't happened through writing or radio or television. It has been a process of inner reflection.

In 2002, two years after the project had officially ended, the team held a half-day reunion. I was impressed by their level of excitement at being back together. At one of the lunch tables, four of the team members sat together, deep in conversation, each of them a presidential candidate for their party. This was a big change from their very first lunch, when each faction had sat separately. Team members had launched several influential new cross-boundary national dialogue groups: one among organizations of the highly fragmented left, another among indigenous organizations, and another among politicians from the twenty different political parties. They had sponsored 200 municipal dialogues (in two-thirds of all municipalities) to address pressing local challenges. Guatemalans were substituting the open way of dialogue for the closed way of force. They were escaping the apartheid syndrome.

The coffee break that afternoon went on for more than an hour, as team members energetically compared notes, offered help, and made fresh plans. The most important result of the project—out of which all the other results flowed—was this trusting web of relationships. Team members said that the project was rejuvenating the country's circulatory system, the life-giving blood vessels connecting different parts of the national body. In a country like Guatemala, where the social fabric has been shredded by conflict, problems cannot be solved until sectoral leaders are able to talk with and listen to each other. I asked one of the project's funders if he thought that his money had been well spent. He looked around at the intersectoral huddles: "This networking alone is worth the money. The most important outcome of this project is the buddy system that was established and persists. The network gets activated immediately, for quite daring initiatives. Perspectives are shared without fear. People are bonded, probably for life."

In the years since the project ended, Guatemala has been on a roller coaster. The 1999 elections brought to power the party led by General Efrain Rios Montt, who had been dictator during the worst years of the genocide. Political violence and repression returned. Against this dark backdrop, Visión Guatemala and its offshoot dialogue processes were hope-generating sources of light: fireflies. Lars Franklin of the United Nations called Visión Guatemala "a positive point of reference for Guatemalans who want to get things back on track." One member of the team said, "It is true that things are not going well now. But without dialogues like Visión Guatemala, we would have already had a military coup." Another said, "When things go badly here, we all dig our trenches deeper. Visión Guatemala gives us bridges across our trenches."

In the run-up to the 2003 elections, Rios Montt orchestrated a terrifying day of riots in Guatemala City to force electoral rules to be changed in his favor. Within two days, an extraordinarily broad coalition of political and civil society organizations had come together to protest, led by members of Visión Guatemala—their network had been activated immediately. In the elections a few months later, Rios Montt came a distant third. When the new government was formed in the beginning of 2004, one-third of the cabinet ministers were members of the team. The fireflies were flying, lit up with hope.

———

Katrin Käufer of the MIT Sloan School of Management led the group of researchers who interviewed members of the Visión Guatemala team. She noticed that the conversations of the Visión Guatemala team map closely onto Otto Scharmer's four different ways of talking and listening.

The first way is downloading: saying what we always say and not listening at all. This is what Elena Diez Pinto was worried about when she saw each group sitting separately and thought, "They're not going to talk with each other. In Guatemala . . . we say 'yes' but we mean 'no.'"

The second way of listening is debating: listening fairly and objectively. This is what the Guatemalan team member was doing when he tried to "actually listen, not to be thinking mentally of how I am going to respond." Listening openly goes along with talking openly, as when "the young man called us 'old pessimists.'"

The third way is talking and listening with empathy, subjectively, from the heart: reflective dialogue. Raquel Zelaya demonstrated this when she listened and then said to General Julio

Balconi, "I know that nobody enrolls in the military academy in order to learn how to massacre women and children."

The fourth way, generative dialogue, was the listening that surrounded Ochaeta's talking—like John Milton's open left hand cupping his loosely clenched right fist. The team sensed that something important and special happened during the storytelling. One story seemed to flow into another, as if the tellers were all telling parts of the same larger story. Time seemed to slow down: I wasn't sure how long the "five minutes" of silence actually lasted. The normal separation between people seemed to lessen: the team shifted from listening to each other's individual perspectives to being, for a while, a whole collective "I."

Two of the team members referred to this experience as being one of "communion." Later I told this story to Robert Stark, a Catholic priest from New Mexico who had spent a lot of time in Guatemala, and asked him how he understood the word "communion" in this context. "I recognize the experience you have described," he said, "as that palpable feeling of our deepest essences being in contact. Communion means a merging of spirit. When we break bread together, we deepen the bonds among us, and when we eat the communion bread, we become one body in Christ. Being in communion is the understanding that we are radically connected. Indigenous people like the Mayans know about this connection. In silence we can feel this connection powerfully: this is the silence of oneness."

Then I realized that I had had that experience of radical connectedness two other times. At my wedding to Dorothy, during our vows, the whole tent full of people had seemed to be one. And when I was alone in the Pyrenees, I had felt one with the immense whole of nature.

When the team had listened to Ochaeta, we were not listening with empathy towards him as an individual. He was, in fact, a peripheral member of the team. The story was not about him and he told it with little emotion. Several other people in the room could have told similar stories from their own experiences.

Instead, Ochaeta's talking was a vehicle on which that critically important story entered the room and was heard by the whole team. In an empathetic conversation (as in Zelaya's with Balconi), each story is a piece of a puzzle, and such a conversation in a diverse group allows the larger picture to become visible. But in this storytelling session, each story was a hologram that contained the whole picture. In Ochaeta's story, the team glimpsed the essence of the whole Guatemalan reality that showed them what they needed to do, which one of them later summarized as: "We must struggle to prevent this from happening again."

Quantum physicist David Bohm once said that the universe is whole but we mistakenly see it as fragmented, as if we are looking in a cracked mirror. In that moment of generative dialogue, the Visión Guatemala team saw the whole.

In their storytelling session, the Visión Guatemala team discovered the source of their shared commitment. They had all signaled their general commitment to the project by coming to that first workshop. But their precise purpose, and the commitment they had to that purpose, only became clear to them during the five minutes of silence. This session occurred during the first meeting of the team, as if this purpose was already present, waiting to be discovered. From their glimpse of the whole of the Guatemalan situation, they knew what they had to do, even though the details of the initiatives they would take to enact the purpose only came later—just as I knew at Mont Fleur that I had to walk through the door that was open, even though I did not know what was on the other side.

My colleagues Peter Senge, Otto Scharmer, Joseph Jaworski, and Betty Sue Flowers call this phenomenon "presence." In *Presence: Human Purpose and the Field of the Future*, they write

> We've come to believe that the core capacity needed for accessing the field of the future is presence. We first thought of presence as being fully conscious and aware in the present moment. Then we began to appreciate presence as deep lis-

tening, of being open beyond one's preconceptions and historical ways of making sense. We came to see the importance of letting go of old identities and the need to control . . . Ultimately, we came to see all aspects of presence as leading to a state of "letting come," of consciously participating in a larger field of change. When this happens, the field shifts, and the forces shaping a situation can shift from re-creating the past to manifesting or realizing an emerging future.

At the conclusion of the Mont Fleur project, one of the team members had given me his thoughtful, qualified assessment of the project. "What we accomplished was to map out in broad terms the successful outcome. We captured the way forward of those of us committed to finding a way forward, and now we are filling it in. But I am uneasy about having compromised on things that matter to me." I had often reflected on this statement and wondered how a group could achieve a kind of agreement that went beyond a compromise.

Then at the conclusion of the Visión Guatemala project, Elena Diez Pinto told me that the sacred book of the Mayan Q'iche people, called the Popol Vuh, contains the following text: "We did not put our ideas together. We put our purposes together. And we agreed, and then we decided." The Visión Guatemala team's presence allowed them to achieve not merely a compromise on ideas but an agreement on purpose. This deep agreement on purpose enabled them to make their important contribution to creating a new and better future for Guatemala.

When Desmond Tutu retired as the Anglican Archbishop of Southern Africa, Njongonkulu Ndungane was elected to replace him. The thirty-two bishops who made up the regional synod were all coming to Cape Town for Ndungane's enthronement, and so he decided to convene a strategic planning workshop. He asked me to facilitate, and fearing that I would not be able to follow the Christian technicalities, I asked Dorothy to work with me. This was the first time we had worked together since Mont Fleur, and we found it a joyous experience. The meeting started and ended each day in church, praying and singing. The group had an exceptionally clear sense of their mission. They also had several long-festering issues that they needed to work through.

The bishops were extraordinarily patient and present listeners. On the first day, we were talking about ground rules for the meeting. One bishop suggested, "We must listen to one another." A second bishop said, "No, brother, that's not quite it. We must listen with empathy." Then a third said, "Brother, that's still not quite what we need. We must listen to the sacred within each of us."

When the Visión Guatemala team listened to Ochaeta's story, they were listening to the sacred. They were listening, through him, to the best that could be in Guatemala and in themselves. To create new and better futures, we must listen to this highest potential in our situations, as it manifests itself within and through each of us.

I told the story of Visión Guatemala to Laura Chasin, Director of Boston's Public Conversations Project, who has facilitated several deep, difficult dialogues, including an extended one between pro-choice and pro-life activists. She was silent for a while. "Your story," she said thoughtfully, "reminds me of something I learned two years ago, when my husband had a terrible accident. He was swimming in a lake and a motorboat ran over him. The propeller cut a gaping gash in his leg. We rushed him to the hospital, but the doctor said that the wound was too large to be sewn up. The only thing we could do was keep the area clean and dry. 'The two sides of the wound will reach out to each other,' the doctor said. 'The wound wants to be whole.'

"The dialogues you and I are involved in are like that," Chasin continued. "The participants and the human systems they are part of want to be whole. Our job as facilitators and leaders is simply to help create a clean, safe space. Then the healing will occur."

Conclusion: An Open Way

*H*OW CAN WE SOLVE our tough problems without resorting to force? How can we overcome the apartheid syndrome in our homes, workplaces, communities and countries, and globally? How can we heal our world's gaping wounds?

The answer to these questions is simple, but it is not easy. We have to bring together the people who are co-creating the current reality to co-create new realities. We have to shift from downloading and debating to reflective and generative dialogue. We have to choose an open way over a closed way.

This injunction to open up is not surprising. Many texts on marriage, management, negotiation, and spirituality give similar advice. What *is* surprising is that when we make this simple, practical shift in how we perform these most basic social actions—talking and listening—we unlock our most complex, stuck problem situations. We create miracles.

How can you get started? Here are ten suggestions:

1. *Pay attention to your state of being and to how you are talking and listening.* Notice your own assumptions, reactions, contractions, anxieties, prejudices, and projections.

2. *Speak up.* Notice and say what you are thinking, feeling, and wanting.

3. *Remember that you don't know the truth about anything.* When you think that you are absolutely certain about the way things are, add "in my opinion" to your sentence. Don't take yourself too seriously.

4. *Engage with and listen to others who have a stake in the system.* Seek out people who have different, even opposing, perspectives from yours. Stretch beyond your comfort zone.

5. *Reflect on your own role in the system.* Examine how what you are doing or not doing is contributing to things being the way they are.

6. *Listen with empathy.* Look at the system through the eyes of the other. Imagine yourself in the shoes of the other.

7. *Listen to what is being said not just by yourself and others but through all of you.* Listen to what is emerging in the system as a whole. Listen with your heart. Speak from your heart.

8. *Stop talking.* Camp out beside the questions and let answers come to you.

9. *Relax and be fully present.* Open up your mind and heart and will. Open yourself up to being touched and transformed.

10. *Try out these suggestions and notice what happens.* Sense what shifts in your relationships with others, with yourself, and with the world. Keep on practicing.

These suggestions are simple but they are far from easy. Most of us—certainly I—fail to follow them most of the time. They are challenging because they require us to make a subtle and fundamental shift in the way we relate to the world. In opening ourselves up, we are lowering our defenses and giving up autonomy and control. We are unclenching our fists and allowing our certainties and identities—our selves—to be challenged and changed.

There is a story about a man who wanted to change the world. He tried as hard as he could, but really did not accomplish anything. So he thought that instead he should just try to change his country, but he had no success with that either. Then he tried to change his city and then his neighborhood, still unsuccessfully. Then he thought that he could at least change his family, but failed again. So he decided to change himself. Then a surprising thing happened. As he changed himself, his family changed too. And as his family changed, his neighborhood changed. As his neighborhood changed, his city changed. As his city changed, his country changed, and as his country changed, the world changed.

How can we change ourselves in this way that allows us to contribute to changing the world? Again, the answer is simple but not easy. We have to practice. To practice meditating, we simply take notice of where our mind is, and continue, over and over, to bring our attention back to our breath. Similarly, to practice opening ourselves up, we simply take notice of how we are, and continue, over and over, to bring our attention back to being present, relaxing, and opening up. Fortunately, we have abundant opportunities to do this practice: including in every conversation, in every context, every day.

This practice and this work are part of a larger emerging movement that is being pioneered by people working in all contexts, at all scales, all over the world. In the early 1990s, when our Shell team looked at what was going on around the world, we came up with two plausible stories about the future: *Barricades,* a scenario characterized by fear, closing down, and fragmentation, and *New Frontiers,* a scenario of hope, opening up, and wholeness. Since then, nearly every group I have worked with has articulated one scenario in which vested interests replay the status quo over and over, in a downward spiral, and another scenario in which a broad, dialogic coalition creates a better reality for all. Everywhere people are struggling to develop a more open and participative way of addressing the immense challenges we face.

Like all pioneering work, the results of this open way are so far uneven. Sometimes they are outstanding and sometimes not. We still have a lot to learn about how to do this well. This will take time and practice. And like all human work, it is not a panacea. "Out of the crooked timber of humanity," philosopher Immanuel Kant wrote, "no straight thing was ever made." But this open way is important, promising, and hopeful.

The greatest gift this work has given me is hope. What inspired me to move to South Africa in 1993, and what continues to inspire me in other settings, is the hope—the noncynicism—of the people who believe they can contribute to creating a better world. In 1998, a journalist asked Czech president Vaclav Havel if he was optimistic or pessimistic about the war in Bosnia. "I am not optimistic," Havel replied, "because I do not believe that everything will turn out well. And I am not pessimistic, because I do not believe that everything will turn out badly. I have hope. Hope is as important as life itself. Without hope we will never reach our dreams."

In late January 2004, I was in India. I spoke with the president of the country's biggest business association, who had just come back from the elite World Economic Forum in Davos, Switzerland. He was hopeful and excited about both global and local trends, and at the same time deeply concerned. "The real problem we have," he said thoughtfully, "is that everyone is talking and nobody is listening. What kind of world are we creating?" Then I spoke with the president of an Indian grassroots organization, who had just come back from the competing, populist World Social Forum in Bombay. "It was a festival of protest against the status quo," he said, shaking his head. "I really believe that, as the slogan of the World Social Forum says, 'Another World Is Possible.' But how can we bring this other world into reality?"

Every one of us gets to choose, in every encounter every day, which world we will contribute to bringing into reality. When we choose the closed way, we participate in creating a world filled with force and fear. When we choose an open way, we participate in creating another, better world.

Notes

14 **Pierre Wack, ... who had invented this approach in the early 1970s.**
See Art Kleiner, *The Age of Heretics: Heroes, Outlaws, and the Forerunners of Corporate Change* (New York: Doubleday, 1996), Peter Schwartz, *The Art of the Long View: Planning for the Future in an Uncertain World* (New York: Currency, 1996), and Kees van der Heijden, *Scenarios: The Art of Strategic Conversation* (West Sussex: John Wiley, 1996).

16 **Economic and political vested interests are deeply threatened by opening up.** Joseph Jaworski, *Synchronicity: The Inner Path of Leadership* (San Francisco: Berrett-Koehler, 1996).

23 *Flight of the Flamingoes* ... **everyone in the society rising slowly and together.** Pieter le Roux et al., "The Mont Fleur Scenarios." *Deeper News*, vol. 7, no. 1 (1992).

25 **Mandela made a decision—the deadlock ... must be broken.** Patti Waldmeir, *Anatomy of a Miracle: The End of Apartheid and the Birth of the New South Africa* (New York: W. W. Norton & Company, 1997), 71.

25 **"The Great U-Turn."** Allister Sparks, *Beyond the Miracle: Inside the New South Africa* (Johannesburg: Jonathan Ball Publishers, 2003), 170.

25 **"if you have internalized something then you probably carry it for life."** Unpublished working paper for Glennifer Gillespie, "The Mont Fleur Scenario Project, South Africa, 1991–1992: The Footprints of Mont Fleur," in *Civic Scenario/Civic Dialogue Workshop*, ed. Bettye Pruitt (New York: United Nations Development Programme Regional Bureau for Latin America and the Caribbean, 2000).

27 **"Using scenarios in this way can be an extraordinarily powerful process."** Jaworski 1996, 182.

30   **"Social capital."** Robert Putnam, *Bowling Alone: The Collapse and Revival of American Community* (New York: Simon & Schuster, 2001).

31   **I knew that problems are tough . . . and that there are three types of complexity: dynamic, generative, and social.** Peter Senge and Claus Otto Scharmer, "Community Action Research," in *Handbook of Action Research*, eds. Peter Reason and Hilary Bradbury (Thousand Oaks, CA: Sage Publications, 2001), 23.

31   **Russell Ackoff calls them "messes."** Russell Ackoff, *Redesigning the Future: A Systems Approach to Societal Problems* (New York: John Wiley and Sons, 1974).

33   **"where the First and Third Worlds meet."** Sparks 2003, x.

41   **"Time and again, conflicts are resolved through shifts that were unimaginable at the start."** Nelson Mandela, "Annual Independent News & Media Lecture" (Dublin, April 12, 2000).

42   **Otto Scharmer calls the kind of talking that takes place in these situations "downloading."** Claus Otto Scharmer, *Theory U: Leading from the Emerging Future* (forthcoming in 2005).

48   **"Dictatorship did not just coerce Chileans; it also corrupted them."** Tina Rosenberg, *Children of Cain: Violence and the Violent in Latin America* (New York: Penguin Books, 1991), 335, 346–47.

51   **"'the rationalist school', . . . codifies thought and action separately."** van der Heijden 1996, 23–24.

62   **This insight made its way into one of the team's published scenarios, *Forward March*.** Alfredo de León and Elena Diez Pinto, "Destino Colombia, 1997–2000: A Treasure to Be Revealed," in *Civic Scenario/Civic Dialogue Workshop*, ed. Bettye Pruitt (New York: United Nations Development Programme Regional Bureau for Latin America and the Caribbean, 2000).

62   **"a treasure still to be revealed."** de León and Diez Pinto, in *Civic Scenario/Civic Dialogue Workshop*, 2000.

75   **"we want the 'whole system' in the room, meaning a larger system than usual."** Marvin Weisbord and Sandra Janoff, *Future Search: An Action Guide to Finding Common Ground in Organizations and Communities* (San Francisco: Berrett-Koehler, 1999), 37–38.

77 "we must listen, discern, and acknowledge this partial truth in everyone—particularly those with whom we disagree." Gene Knudsen Hoffman, "Compassionate Listening: A First Step Towards Reconciliation," in *Compassionate Listening Training: An Exploratory Sourcebook about Conflict Transformation,* by Gene Knudsen Hoffman, Cynthia Monroe, and Leah Green, ed. Dennis Rivers (Santa Barbara: The Institute for Cooperative Communication Skills, 2001), 2.

80 They "suspended" their ideas, . . . and walked around and looked at these ideas from different perspectives. See William Isaacs, *Dialogue and the Art of Thinking Together* (New York: Doubleday, 1999).

80 "You had time to think . . . to see the contradictions in yourself." Anthony Sampson, *Mandela: An Authorized Biography* (New York: Alfred A. Knopf, 1999), xxvi.

80 "we had to *carve* it, and so perhaps we were more willing to listen." This and all the indented quotes in this chapter from Gillespie 2000.

84 "cognition is not a representation of an independent, pregiven world." Fritjof Capra, *The Web of Life: A New Scientific Understanding of Living Systems* (New York: Doubleday, 1996), 270. See also Humberto Maturana and Francisco Varela, *The Tree of Knowledge: The Biological Roots of Human Understanding* (Boston: Shambhala, 1987).

85 "some of us were reluctant to say we worked for Shell." Cor Herströter, Mark Moody-Stuart, and Gary Steel, "Strategic Transformation at Royal Dutch/Shell," in *The Dance of Change: The Challenges of Sustaining Momentum in Learning Organizations,* eds. Peter Senge et al. (New York: Doubleday, 1999), 527–528.

89 "Sawu bona," which means "I see you." Peter Senge et al., eds., *The Fifth Discipline Fieldbook: Strategies and Tools for Building a Learning Organization* (New York: Doubleday, 1994), 3.

90 "I am *genuinely* interested in him! That's the whole point!" See Joseph Jaworski, "When Good People Do Terrible Things: Addressing the Fundamental Learning Impediments of Organizational Life," in *The Dance of Change.*

91 He was developing a taxonomy of four different ways of listening. Scharmer forthcoming.

97 **"or you can sit together and work through a solution yourselves."** "Interview of Adam Kahane: 'In Today's Argentina, the Options Are Dialogue or Violence,'" *La Nación* (Buenos Aires), 5 May 2002.

99 **"An experiment never before tried in our country has just started up."** Editorial, "Judicial Reform and Dialogue," *La Nación* (Buenos Aires), 30 September 2002.

109 **"Instead, we rely on patterns—and on feelings associated with those patterns."** Brian Arthur, "Unit of One: Decisions, Decisions," *Fast Company* (October 1998): 93.

113 **The official, internationally supported investigation of this period was the "Commission for Historical Clarification."** Commission for Historical Clarification, *Guatemala Memory of Silence: Report of the Commission for Historical Clarification* (Washington, D.C.: American Association for the Advancement of Science, 1999).

114 **"I was worried that we would be so polite that the real issues would never emerge."** This and all other indented quotes in this chapter from Elena Diez Pinto, "Visión Guatemala, 1998–2000: Building Bridges of Trust," in *Civic Scenario/Civic Dialogue Workshop.*

122 **Katrin Käufer . . . led the group of researchers who interviewed members of the Visión Guatemala team.** Katrin Käufer, "Learning from Civic Scenario Projects: A Tool for Facilitating Social Change?" in *Civic Scenario/Civic Dialogue Workshop.*

125 **"We've come to believe that the core capacity needed for accessing the field of the future is presence."** Peter Senge, Claus Otto Scharmer, Joseph Jaworski, and Betty Sue Flowers, *Presence: Human Purpose and the Field of the Future* (Cambridge: Society for Organizational Learning, 2004), 11.

132 **Immanuel Kant.** Quoted in Isaiah Berlin, *The Crooked Timber of Humanity: Chapters in the History of Ideas* (Princeton: Princeton University Press, 1990), ii.

132 **Czech president Vaclav Havel.** Quoted by Thorvald Stoltenberg, the former UN envoy to Bosnia, at the Tallberg Conference, 1998.

Bibliography

Ackoff, Russell, *Redesigning the Future: A Systems Approach to Societal Problems*. New York: John Wiley and Sons, 1974.

Arthur, Brian, "Unit of One: Decisions, Decisions." *Fast Company* (October 1998).

Berlin, Isaiah, *The Crooked Timber of Humanity: Chapters in the History of Ideas*. Princeton: Princeton University Press, 1990.

Bohm, David, and Mark Edwards, *Changing Consciousness: Exploring the Hidden Source of the Social, Political, and Environmental Crises Facing Our World*. New York: HarperCollins, 1991.

Capra, Fritjof, *The Web of Life: A New Scientific Understanding of Living Systems*. New York: Doubleday, 1996.

Carvajal, Manuel Jose, et al., "Destino Colombia." *Deeper News*, vol. 9, no. 1 (1998).

Commission for Historical Clarification, *Guatemala Memory of Silence: Report of the Commission for Historical Clarification*. Washington, D.C.: American Association for the Advancement of Science, 1999.

Diez Pinto, Elena, et al., *Los Escenarios del Futuro*. Guatemala City: Visión Guatemala, 1999.

Hoffman, Gene Knudsen, Cynthia Monroe, and Leah Green, edited by and with an introduction by Dennis Rivers, *Compassionate Listening Training: An Exploratory Sourcebook about Conflict Transformation*. Santa Barbara: The Institute for Cooperative Communication Skills, 2001.

Isaacs, William, *Dialogue and the Art of Thinking Together*. New York: Doubleday, 1999.

Jaworski, Joseph, *Synchronicity: The Inner Path of Leadership.* San Francisco: Berrett-Koehler, 1996.

Kleiner, Art, *The Age of Heretics: Heroes, Outlaws, and the Forerunners of Corporate Change.* New York: Doubleday, 1996.

le Roux, Pieter, et al., "The Mont Fleur Scenarios." *Deeper News,* vol. 7, no. 1 (1992).

Maturana, Humberto, and Francisco Varela, *The Tree of Knowledge: The Biological Roots of Human Understanding.* Boston: Shambhala, 1987.

Owen, Harrison, *Open Space Technology.* San Francisco: Berrett-Koehler, 1998.

Pruitt, Bettye, ed., *Civic Scenario/Civic Dialogue Workshop.* New York: United Nations Development Programme Regional Bureau for Latin America and the Caribbean, 2000.

Putnam, Robert, *Bowling Alone: The Collapse and Revival of American Community.* New York: Simon & Schuster, 2001.

Reason, Peter, and Hilary Bradbury, eds., *Handbook of Action Research.* Thousand Oaks, CA: Sage Publications, 2001.

Rosenberg, Tina, *Children of Cain: Violence and the Violent in Latin America.* New York: Penguin Books, 1991.

Sampson, Anthony, *Mandela: An Authorized Biography.* New York: Alfred A. Knopf, 1999.

Scharmer, Claus Otto, *Theory U: Leading from the Emerging Future.* Forthcoming in 2005.

Scharmer, Claus Otto, Brian Arthur, Jonathon Day, Joseph Jaworski, Michael Jung, Ikujiro Nonaka, and Peter Senge, "Illuminating the Blind Spot." *Leader to Leader* (spring 2002): 11–14.

Schwartz, Peter, *The Art of the Long View: Planning for the Future in an Uncertain World.* New York: Currency, 1996.

Senge, Peter, Claus Otto Scharmer, Joseph Jaworski, and Betty Sue Flowers, *Presence: Human Purpose and the Field of the Future.* Cambridge: Society for Organizational Learning, 2004.

Senge, Peter, Art Kleiner, Charlotte Roberts, Richard Ross, and Bryan Smith, eds., *The Fifth Discipline Fieldbook: Strategies and Tools for Building a Learning Organization.* New York: Doubleday, 1994.

Senge, Peter, Art Kleiner, Charlotte Roberts, Richard Ross, George Roth, and Bryan Smith, *The Dance of Change: The Challenges of Sustaining Momentum in Learning Organizations.* New York: Doubleday, 1999.

Sparks, Allister, *Beyond the Miracle: Inside the New South Africa.* Johannesburg: Jonathan Ball Publishers, 2003.

van der Heijden, Kees, *Scenarios: The Art of Strategic Conversation.* West Sussex: John Wiley, 1996.

Waldmeir, Patti, *Anatomy of a Miracle: The End of Apartheid and the Birth of the New South Africa.* New York: W. W. Norton & Company, 1997.

Weisbord, Marvin, and Sandra Janoff, *Future Search: An Action Guide to Finding Common Ground in Organizations and Communities.* San Francisco: Berrett-Koehler, 1999.

Index

About the Author

*A*DAM KAHANE is a founding partner (with Joseph Jaworski and Bill O'Brien) of Generon Consulting, and of the Global Leadership Initiative. He is a leading designer and facilitator of processes through which business, government, and civil society leaders can work together to solve their toughest, most complex problems. He has worked in this area in more than fifty countries, in every part of the world, with executives and politicians, generals and guerrillas, civil servants and trade unionists, community activists and United Nations officials, journalists and clergy, academics and artists.

During the early 1990s, Adam was head of Social, Political, Economic and Technological Scenarios for Royal Dutch/Shell in London. Previously he held strategy and research positions with Pacific Gas and Electric Company (San Francisco), the Organisation for Economic Cooperation and Development (Paris), the International Institute for Applied Systems Analysis (Vienna), the Institute for Energy Economics (Tokyo), and the Universities of Toronto, British Columbia, California, and the Western Cape.

In 1991 and 1992, Adam facilitated the Mont Fleur Scenario Project, in which a diverse group of South Africans worked together to effect the transition to democracy. Since then he has led many such seminal multi-stakeholder dialogue-and-action processes throughout the world. He was one of the sixteen outstanding individuals featured in *Fast Company's* first annual "Who's Fast" and is a member of the Commission on Globalisation, the Aspen Institute's Business Leaders' Dialogue, the Society for Organizational Learning, and Global Business Network.

Adam has a B.Sc. in Physics (First Class Honors) from McGill University (Montreal), an M.A. in Energy and Resource Economics from the University of California (Berkeley), and an M.A. in Applied Behavioral Science from Bastyr University (Seattle). He has also studied negotiation at Harvard Law School and cello performance at Institut Marguerite-Bourgeoys.

Originally from Montreal, he lives in Boston and Cape Town with his wife Dorothy and their family.

Generon Consulting
900 Cummings Center, Suite 312U
Beverly, Massachusetts 01915
United States of America
www.generonconsulting.com
kahane@generonconsulting.com

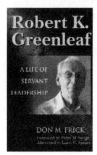
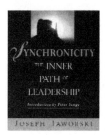